Andrew Sneddon is co-owner and a director of Australia's largest specialist heritage consultancy. He has lived and worked in Melbourne and Sydney, and been involved in archaeological research excavations around the world, including in Cyprus, Syria, Türkiye, Uzbekistan, Italy, Greece, Cambodia and Myanmar. Andrew was the Director of UQ's Culture and Heritage Unit from 2009 to 2017. He currently lives in Brisbane with his wife and son. *Prehistoric Joy* is his first book.

Pre HISTORIC JOY

A MEMOIR

ANDREW SNEDDON

UQP

First published 2023 by University of Queensland Press
PO Box 6042, St Lucia, Queensland 4067 Australia

University of Queensland Press (UQP) acknowledges the Traditional Owners and their
custodianship of the lands on which UQP operates. We pay our respects to their Ancestors
and their descendants, who continue cultural and spiritual connections to Country. We
recognise their valuable contributions to Australian and global society.

uqp.com.au
reception@uqp.com.au

Cover design by Josh Durham (Design by Committee)
Illustrations by Andrew Sneddon
Author photograph by Walter Kennard
Typeset in 12.5/17 pt Adobe Garamond Pro by Post Pre-press Group, Brisbane
Printed in Australia by McPherson's Printing Group

 **Queensland Government** University of Queensland Press is supported by the Queensland
Government through Arts Queensland.

 **Australia Council for the Arts** University of Queensland Press is assisted by the
Australian Government through the Australia
Council, its arts funding and advisory body.

A catalogue record for this book is available from the National Library of Australia.

ISBN 978 0 7022 6615 7 (pbk)
ISBN 978 0 7022 6777 2 (epdf)
ISBN 978 0 7022 6778 9 (epub)

University of Queensland Press uses papers that are natural, renewable and recyclable
products made from wood grown in well-managed forests and other controlled sources.
The logging and manufacturing processes conform to the environmental regulations of the
country of origin.

For Joanne and Patrick

Homer's 2750-year-old epic, *The Iliad*, is a violent poem about the gods and heroes of the Trojan War – a horror show of blood and brains spattered on battlefields. But 'Book I' concludes with a domestic scene. Well, at least, 'a domestic'; an argument between a husband and his wife. Zeus, the Lord of Olympus, accuses his wife, Hera, of being nagging and suspicious. He reminds her that if he wanted to, he could lace his powerful fingers around her elegant, feminine throat and strangle the very life out of her. A son intervenes – the crippled Hephaestus – to console and cajole. He counsels his mother to shut her mouth, and instead of arguing, to mollify the man who beats her. He recalls for her how these things always end, all those times that he has found her broken, bruised and battered. And he remembers the time when he did try to defend her, when he put his body between his mother and his father's wrath, when Zeus took him by the heel and hurled him furiously from the highest peak of Olympus. That time, the son tumbled through the air, through clouds and eddies, past rocky outcrops. Nobody could save him. He was alone. He fell like a stone – for a full day, and into the night.

1. Exit Dad, Stage Right

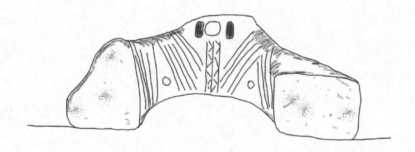

Anthropomorphised hearth, Cyprus, c1750 BCE

I can remember everything else about that afternoon, but I have no clear recollection of why my mother put me in a car with Bevan when I was twelve years old. Bevan was okay, I suppose – a friend of the family, an alcoholic and a noted drink driver. I do remember that we ended up at the Anglers Arms Hotel, which back then was located on a sleepy edge of the Southport Broadwater on Queensland's Gold Coast. It is probably the site of a fancy high-rise building now, but when we were kids it was just a brick box where you could buy cheap beer. It had an enormous cartoon fish made of bright blue neon lights attached to the exterior wall. The fish's mouth flashed open and closed at night, sparkling off the rippled surface of the bay. I think it was probably saying: *Please God, get me out of here.*

That afternoon, against the immutable laws of physics, Bevan got me to the pub safely. As we walked inside together, a tableful of ageing regulars who were deep in a drinking session called us over. I took a seat next to a sixty-year-old woman with vertical smoker's lines on her upper lip and a voice made ragged by tobacco. As Bevan went to the bar to neck a quick pot, I became aware of something: these people knew me. Or at least, they knew *of* me. The woman looked at me with rum-tinctured eyes and I was grateful when one of the blokes offered to buy me a soft drink with a wink and an *it'll-be-okay* thumbs-up. I slipped a hand under each thigh and hunched into the room's hubbub, becoming faintly aware that these people pitied me. When my lemon squash came, the lady next to me told me that I didn't have to worry, because if things got any worse for me at home she had room on the floor of her caravan – you know, if I needed somewhere to sleep. I thanked her and she patted my knee reassuringly. It was all very nice. But I was old enough by now to know that if a drunk, ciggie-smoking retiree in a shitty pub on the Gold Coast thought things were so bad that I might need a place to sleep on the floor of her tiny caravan, then my home life must have been going seriously wrong.

And it was.

*

I once excavated a beautiful 3800-year-old hearth in the home of a prehistoric settlement in Cyprus. Its plaster surrounds formed a horseshoe shape and were incised with dashes, zigzags and two rounded knobs like eyes that made the whole thing look oddly human. That Cypriot hearth was clearly the focus of life in the residence, and not just because it was the place where food was prepared. In a purpose-built niche behind the hearth the occupants of the house had placed a figurine made out of clay and coated with incised plaster, crudely depicting the head and chest of a human being. In the ashy deposits in front of the hearth we recovered a second human figurine, two loom weights, a spindle whorl, a copper needle and two seashells pierced to make jewellery. The hearth and those finds together comprised a moving domestic tableau. Hearth. Home.

The hearth has long been a special place. The ancient Romans regarded it as the pervading and protective spirit of the household, and the goddess of the hearth, Hestia, was revered. The Greeks, too, saw the hearth as the spiritual hub of the home, a sentient presence embodying great power and significance, so much so that the Greek poet Hesiod wrote in the eighth century BCE that men should always show the hearth the utmost respect, as though it was another person in their home, and never be naked when in its presence.

For the prehistoric Cypriots, and for the ancient Greeks and Romans, the hearth seems to have represented security, comfort, sustenance and family – the kind of joy that you can only feel with a full stomach and no fear for what the morning might bring. *La dolce vita*. The sweet life. The good life.

On the cusp of becoming a teenager, at the Anglers Arms Hotel with Bevan, the complexities of my family situation were starting to dawn on me. And not in a good way. Life was anything but sweet. We had moved in and out of so many houses I was starting to lose count. What I didn't know at the time was that being powerless shapes your personality. It makes you watchful, a careful observer of moods and behaviours. You become zebra-on-the-savanna twitchy. You think about people a lot, about how they behave. And if being powerless makes you jumpy, then being poor makes you envious. You notice when other people are happy and you become keenly aware of those things that they have, that make them happy, that you do not have. Sometimes, you know better than they do about what brings them joy. As a kid, to me it seemed pretty simple: the sweet life included a stable home life with a roof over your head, good food, friends and family who loved you. It is a kind of blessedness that the ancient Greeks called *olbios*. As Solon – the Athenian poet and lawgiver – said around 560 BCE, *olbios* is having loving children, horses and hounds, and a hospitable friend you can call on.

As an archaeologist it is rewarding to look for signs and symbols of happiness in those times that predate written history – prehistoric joy. It's better to look for the smiles, the kindness, the *olbios*. It's in there, buried under the layers of dirt, sometimes cheek-by-jowl with the skeletons and spearheads, just waiting for someone to dig it up. In contrast, most archaeologists are more interested in how much people of the past have suffered. They love a good skull fracture. They get very excited when they find arthritis in prehistoric knees. I have lost track of the number of academic texts that begin by quoting Hobbes' line about the lives of prehistoric humans being 'solitary, poor, nasty, brutish, and short'. Nobody ever quotes his footnote about the cuddles! If you doubt me, think of poor Ötzi the Iceman whose body was recovered from the Alps on the Austrian and Italian border in 1991. The crack team of archaeologists and physical anthropologists deployed to analyse the remains had identified the parasites in his lower intestines before they'd even found the arrowhead that killed him wedged in his thoracic cavity!

There's no doubt that life in prehistory – before reading and writing, before antibiotics and anaesthesia – could be very tough. Our forebears had to live with gut parasites and were often emaciated by tapeworms. People died younger than they do today, were hungrier, thinner and buried with fewer teeth in their heads. In a wet winter or mosquito-ridden spring, it's likely a kip on a caravan floor would have been very appealing to them, although they may have drawn the line at a drink in the Anglers Arms in the 1980s.

But I like to think, despite this, our ancestors still would have enjoyed a catchy tune and a cheery fireside chat. Despite longer and harder physical working days, I imagine small communities of friends and family sitting around at mealtimes in little hamlets and villages – laughing, teasing, child-wrangling and storytelling. Even in the most dreadful of circumstances, people will always seek out joy.

*

My own childhood didn't start badly. I was born into a normal working-class family. Mum grew up in a small country town that didn't have a high school, so she repeated the last year of primary school, then with nothing else to do she taught herself how to type and ended up a secretary in the Department of Theoretical Physics at a university in Canberra. My father left school in country New South Wales at the age of fifteen and became an apprentice butter maker, a career choice that, unsurprisingly, did not result in fame and riches. Rather, armed with a butter pat, he started work in one of Australia's largest commercial dairies, only to end up getting sacked for being argumentative. Ultimately, he landed a job in the Australian National University, assisting professors to research forms of mosquito-borne encephalitis.

In suburban Canberra, the secretary and dairy technologist married and made a life for themselves, initially surrounded by an assortment of professional astrophysicists and entomologists. Mum and Dad saved some money and together opened a suburban dress shop. For a brief time, we were like any middle-class family, which was terrific at Christmas time and birthdays when the loot rolled in. But with insecurities as big as theirs, my parents' relationship was always on a downward trajectory. They should have been proud of themselves, dragging themselves up from humble beginnings and all that, but instead they hobbled around under the weight of enormous chips on their shoulders and argued unrelentingly. This wasn't the petty bickering that many couples inevitably face; instead, theirs involved screaming personal abuse, door slamming and nagging, followed by rage-filled silences. There were *no* concessions. My parents would disagree about the merits and value of super glue as an adhesive for everyday use, with a particular focus on the chances of my four-year-old sister gluing herself to the washing machine. They argued about the most desirable consistency of gravy like some people argued about Brexit – sleeping on it, stewing on it and then reigniting the same argument days later. They even argued about whether the fridge setting was appropriate for butter spreadability (Dad was qualified, remember!).

Then, one afternoon when I was almost nine, my mother told us kids – me, my older brother, John, and younger sister, Sophie – to pack our pyjamas, toothbrushes and a change of undies into our pillowcases, because we were going to spend the night at our grandparents' place. We had stayed with Nana and Papa before, and I thought nothing of it. In my diary, I wrote: *today wasn't very exciting*.

But it was the last time I would live in the same house as my father. Exit Dad, stage right.

After Mum and Dad separated, a vicious custody battle followed. First, there were marriage counsellors, then there were therapists who sat with us three children to gently ask, over and again, why it was that we kept saying that we didn't want to see our father anymore. There *must* be a reason, they would say. I told them what my mother had coached me to tell them. None of it felt real, not the counselling sessions after school or the daytrips to Dad's house where he had 'custody' for four hours every few weeks.

Then, in the middle of my parents' separation, my grandfather died. My mother adored him, and on top of the separation his loss was devastating for her. Mum was bereft, lost at sea, and just weeks later she washed up on the shore of an English grifter named Philip, who instantly recognised in her the things that some men are finely attuned to – insecurity, loneliness, vulnerability and, in my mother's case, a middle-class income. She was also a bit nuts, which helped.

And so, one year and a day after Mum separated from my father, she was married to my stepfather, Philip. A prick.

Not for one moment did we ever consider calling him 'Dad'.

2. So Much For Luck

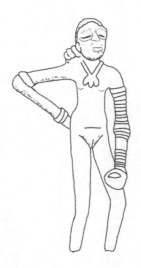

'The Dancing Girl', Mohenjo-Daro, Pakistan,
2300–1750 BCE

I know that I had a life before I met the man who would become my stepfather, a childhood full of childhood stuff, but it all seems dim and murky to me. It is like I entered the world a fully formed almost ten-year-old, emerging from the loins of a mustard-yellow late-1970s Holden Torana in suburban Canberra. It was when Philip appeared, drunk and belligerent, that my new life began.

Philip was forty years old when that happened, a man of medium height and build, save for his belly which strained his belt somewhat, with jet-black hair and a swarthy complexion. He was born in India, in the terminal days of the British Empire, apportioned two 'native' nannies for the first few years of his life, and although his mother denied it vehemently, he was clearly part-Indian, something that attracted cruel, racist teasing at the public-school boarding house in England that he was sent to as a young lad. His left leg was a little shorter

13

than his right, and he walked with a slight limp, another focus for bullying in a boarding school in the 1950s. He had a round face and dark hooded eyes. He was always watchful, alert, a little jumpy. When we went out to dinner, I would catch him glancing at the restaurant's entrance like he was expecting trouble. If my mother walked to the bathroom, he would watch her coldly, as if she was trying to make an escape or might talk to somebody she wasn't supposed to. He was outwardly prone to giggles, but his eyes never laughed. He wasn't big, but he was bigger than Mum.

Their courtship was brief, to say the least. Most of the wooing took place in the Australian Alps, a couple of hours drive from Canberra, in a nasty brick-veneer, single-storey house near Lake Jindabyne. Where the backdrop could have been frost and snow it was bone dry eucalypt forest, the long summer days and warm evenings either side of Christmas. I don't know who owned the house, but it seemed to be in the care of a man named Graham 'Saliva' McGyvar, who slipped in and out of the bedroom with his girlfriend, Brenda, making sex jokes and burping. There was also a friend who lived in a Kombi van out the back with his dog, Wart. These names alone should have raised some very big red flags for Mum. We were entering unfamiliar, tawdry territory but she was clearly falling in love and love is proverbially blind. For example, it was blind to an unselfconscious Brenda sitting on the front of Graham's sparkly blue speed boat with her boobs out as it shot across Lake Jindabyne. Philip was on his best behaviour, rationing his booze and keeping a lid on his anger.

That New Year's Eve the neighbours who lived in a house hundreds of metres away, through scraggy gum trees and dusty sunlight, invited us over for schnapps. They were an elderly German couple who had emigrated to Australia after the war, and finding something familiar in the Australian ski fields, they had settled. Before we left that night, the couple insisted that John, Sophie and I climb the loft of their old barn and ring the cow bells that they had hung from the rafters. It was an old German tradition, they told us, and it would bring us luck. It was way past our bedtime as we clunked the hollow bells and then carefully descended the creaky timber ladder, with Mum crying out, 'Be careful kids!' I remember walking back home in a daze, dry gum leaves crunching underfoot, moonlight filtering through tree branches and whirring insects overhead. Mum and Philip were walking a little ahead of us, chatting quietly. Looking back over the five years that were to follow, I can honestly say that this is the only happy memory I have of being in his company.

It was in that brick-veneer house one morning near Lake Jindabyne, with Wart chasing a tennis ball behind the garage, Brenda spread-eagled on a deck chair in her bikini and sipping a glass of chardonnay, and Saliva McGyvar tooling with the outboard on his speed boat, that Mum told us she and Philip were engaged. John cried. Later, he and I slipped outside and stood by the side of the house to talk it over. Mum had spent almost a year leading up to that point turning us against our real father, telling us he was selfish, cruel and unfeeling. She had coached us in how to call him names on the phone and to berate him for treating her badly. I had parroted those words for her, not ever believing them, but playing my role and waiting for the curtains to be lowered again so that we could take a bow and bask in our applause, expecting zero real-world repercussions. It always felt like things would blow over. We would move back home and our lives would go back to normal – Sunday morning breakfasts with Dad, school drop-offs with Dad and the usual endless arguing.

But suddenly all that changed. We were to have a new father – we were told he would technically be a 'stepfather'. He had been divorced before and had two daughters from that marriage – 'stepsisters' now, we were told. Philip had no visible means of support. He hung out with topless women and men called Saliva and dogs called Wart and drank lots of beer.

Meanwhile, back in our Canberra backyard, my dead grandfather's greenhouse – his place of sanctuary where he had grown giant, red tomatoes and gorgeous flowers – grew saggy and derelict, its thick plastic walls tearing and flapping in the wind. His little terrier, Aussie, suddenly died, which saw Mum in the kitchen that her father had made a thousand cups of tea in, crying into her hands. I realise now that the last vestiges of something were disintegrating for her, she was desperate to build something new to cherish. That may be why her second marriage smacked of unseemly haste.

A few weeks before the wedding I walked in on Mum and Philip having an earnest conversation in Mum's bedroom. Surprisingly, when I asked, Mum told me what they were talking about. A woman had sent Mum an anonymous letter warning her not to marry Philip. The letter said that he was a violent conman. Mum pointed to a light blue envelope on the dresser, and I regret to this day not picking it up and reading it. But as I tuned in to the conversation, I realised that it was actually a bitch session between Mum and Philip about how evil, jealous and spiteful some women can be. Not how correct they might be, or how the sorority might look out for its own. Mum ignored the letter. It was a bad call.

*

It was not a big wedding, but then big weddings aren't for everyone. Small weddings aren't for everyone either. In some cultures, the lifelong bond between husband and wife was solemnised by the simple act of holding hands and jumping over a broom handle together. In others, the woman would simply pack a little bundle of her belongings and move in with her new partner and his family to indicate that they had entered into a state of holy matrimony. Mostly, throughout recorded history, humans have favoured monogamy over the alternatives. Where polygamy was preferred, it was almost always of the one-husband-several-wives variety. Some archaeologists believe that they can discern these relationships in the form and layout of houses, but I doubt it. How would you distinguish a polygamous household from a monogamous one? Would you find houses with one big bedroom full of blokey things and lots of little ones full of perfume bottles? Or one big bedroom with a single enormous bed in the middle of it? And how would you distinguish these things from what Julius Caesar described in Late Iron Age Britain? When Caesar invaded in 55–54 BCE, dodging spears hurled at him by naked celts stained blue with woad, he noted that back in their villages small groups of the local men would just share their enthusiastic wives.

In Mum's mind, the wedding was always going to be the start of a durable, monogamous, loving relationship binding a man and a woman till death did them part. Australian men's fashion at the time was peaking with the safari suit. John got a light brown one and I got a blue one to wear to the wedding. To this day, I consider it the finest piece of clothing that I have ever possessed, and I recall feeling very grown up when trying it on in the store, the trousers cinched with a belt wider than my own thigh.

The ceremony was held without irony in a church, presumably to appease Philip's mother, Millicent, who was very religious, except when ignoring her son's outrageous moral transgressions. My grandmother boycotted the whole thing. Even though Mum had quite a circle of friends, there were not many people in attendance, a clear indication that they were embarrassed to be seen to be taking sides between my mother and father. It was literally twenty-four hours after their divorce was formalised. For Mum, this was a symbolic act, and another humiliation for my father. But there was a whiff of tension on the day. It was understood that Philip would not be driving to the church and he would not drive home from the reception either. He did not drive anywhere, in fact, because just before meeting Mum, he had been charged and convicted of Driving Under the Influence and was disqualified from driving. In the first few weeks of our acquaintance, Philip would disappear at weekends to perform community service, a strange thing that I queried Mum about. She brushed it off as a silly misunderstanding.

They honeymooned on the Hawkesbury River in a rented houseboat. When John, Sophie and I joined them on board during the last few days, we found ourselves suddenly in a confined space with Philip. He seemed restless at times. He would giggle a lot, a laugh that always sounded like embarrassment to me. Shortly after we joined them, Philip moored the boat outside a small town and rowed ashore in driving rain to place a bet on a 'sure thing' a mate had told him about. He came back a couple of hours later, water-logged and beery. More red flags.

After the honeymoon, ashore again in our tiny house in Canberra, Philip came to stay. It was a perplexing development because nothing had ever seemed permanent about him, except perhaps, his criminal record. In fact, Philip had a criminal history which, after the wedding, he was oddly upfront about, even a little boastful of. Mostly it was petty larceny, the work of a conman, a swindler. He would snicker about the old woman he had fleeced of her savings, telling us how easily she was persuaded to part with her money. It was always the same concoction of half-truths and shameless flattery that did the trick, and mostly it was honest people who naively trusted him. He thought nothing of deceit, was immune to empathy. But there was a dark seam of violence, too, a kind of tar that seeped out after a few drinks. It was at the core of him, sticking to him and to us.

Much later, a lifelong friend of Philip's from high school, Bob, told us about a woman in New Zealand who a younger Philip had been in a relationship with. At the time, Bob was living in England when he received a telegram from Philip in New Zealand. Philip had bought a ticket home and begged Bob to pick him up at the airport. When Bob showed up, as requested, Philip emerged through Customs a physical wreck – drunk, scared and jabbering. Incredibly, he was wearing only one shoe. The mysterious girlfriend in New Zealand had 'disappeared' and the woman's family had reported it to police. Philip's explanation was that she was fine, there was nothing to worry about, she had just gone into hiding to get away from him for a bit.

If we take that at face value, if we dig no deeper, it still says nothing good for Philip. It says that people fled from him, families were torn apart by him, reports were made to the police about him, women were afraid of him.

So much for ringing cow bells on New Year's Eve. So much for luck.

3. A Nice House with Nice Things in It

Houses and 'Tree of Life' motif, Domuztepe,
Türkiye, c7000 BCE

In prehistory, people were house-proud. At Neolithic Kalavasos in Cyprus, in 7000 BCE, people lived in tiny circular homes no more than three or four metres in diameter, barely wide enough for even a short person to stretch out and yawn. The village survives today as a series of circular stone footings with mudbrick walls to a height of a metre or so. The little round houses cluster together on a hilltop so that the survey plans of the site look like someone rested a coffee cup on a blank piece of paper, leaving dozens of circular stains. The houses were crammed together, edges touching. There can have been no privacy for sleeping, a quiet conversation or for making love, although privacy is a flexible concept – very popular in modern times where personal space is at a premium. A visit to the public toilets that survive from ancient Rome, where people voided their bowels into a toilet next to another twenty or so people casually doing the same thing, is a good example of how prudish western views today differ from those of the ancient past.

In any event, even in this tiny, cluttered village, somebody 9000 years ago took the time to crush up some coloured minerals into a powder, moisten it and paint a human figure on the inside wall of one of the rooms. The image looks a bit like Bart Simpson and, frankly, leaves a lot to be desired in terms of technical proficiency, but the point is the painter felt the need to jazz the place up a bit. It was home.

Ah, yes. Home sweet home. My mother and Philip liked houses so much that we lived in twelve of them over the course of a few years. The number is so high because although Philip liked houses, he didn't much like paying the rent on them. In fact, he resented it. As a result, we missed out on all of the good things about having a home. We never had the chance to grow to love one, to put down roots there, to fill it with happy memories. Instead, we learned how to slink about in shame when frustrated landlords came by demanding unpaid rent, and to say: 'Mum's not home.' We never really got the chance to unpack because the next move was never far away. It was a topsy-turvy existence completely lacking any kind of stability.

When I first started studying archaeology, I loved the pyramids and the pantheon. I was intrigued by the swords with exotic gemstones inlaid on the hilt and the gold torques. It wasn't until much later that I realised that those things, while fascinating, tell us very little about the vast bulk of humanity, the ninety-nine per cent who were not buried in a pyramid and didn't worship in a domed temple. Throughout the course of human history almost everybody ate dinner by tearing the meat straight off the bone and, later, off a wooden board or ceramic plate. They shat into a hole dug in the ground near where they consumed their food. And so, to really understand how prehistoric people lived, we have to delve into their cesspits and carefully excavate their cooking hearths. We need to make ourselves at home. I have been filled with a sense of reverence crouching in front of a 4000-year-old hearth and tickling the ashy deposits with a trowel, looking much as the owner did all those millennia ago when they cooked dinner in it.

Making sense of the evidence from prehistory, however, is not so easy. The artefacts can be strangely mute. There are no books to read, no written poems or music to shed light on what prehistoric cultures were like. We are left to view the banqueting hall through a keyhole. One of the big challenges is how to interpret the significance of seemingly random things, partly because we humans often see what we want to see. The Chichibu Chinsekikan, or Hall of Curious Rocks, perfectly illustrates this point. This private museum in Japan houses a quirky collection of rocks that resemble human faces. If a person wants to see a face in a perfectly natural lump of stone, they will see it.

But an archaeologist digging up any one of my childhood homes 1000 years hence would not have a clue about what my life was like, or what I was thinking at the time.

*

The first house that I shared with Philip was in Du Faur Street, in the Canberra suburb of Mawson. It was a tiny three-bedroom brick number that at its peak was home to my mother, her brother (my Uncle John), my Nana and Papa, my brother, my sister and me. It must have been incredibly cramped, but I don't remember it that way. I think of it as a place of warmth and happiness. Papa was a bee-keeper and I can still see the huge aluminium containers of honey that he stored in the laundry, slick brown tongues of it slowly pouring over the rim and into jars on cool mornings; I can still taste the exotic curry and rice that Nana would treat us to on Friday nights, although I now know it was just a stew with Keen's curry powder and sultanas thrown in. I played soccer on Saturdays, chased white cabbage moths off Papa's garden on Sundays, walked to the school just up the road on Mondays. It was a childhood full of *Little House on the Prairie* and *The Six Million Dollar Man*. I was obsessed with The Hardy Boys Mystery Stories. Life was pretty good.

Except for the arguing that became a kind of elevator music to my young life – venomous shrieks, violent door slamming, uncontrolled sobs of outrage. The vitriolic fights were a series of sudden flare-ups founded in, and nurtured by, ancient resentments within my mother's family. The resentments worked like peat fire, always there but hot under the surface, licks of yellow flame in buried seams hungrily sniffing out oxygen. There were many reasons for the arguments but they usually involved deep-seated insecurities. My mother would argue with Nana about Uncle John and Uncle John would scream in self-defence and Nana would shriek, 'Leave him alone, you know he can't handle stress.' Mum would shriek back, 'You always take his side,' and slam doors. Nana would complain – 'All this arguing is going to kill me' – and she'd pop blood pressure pills like they were jellybeans. When Papa was alive he would withdraw to his study on the brink of tears and Nana would say, 'Now look what you've done to your father.' Mum would come out of her room with pink cheeks, looking chagrined and everyone would console Papa, and then there would be a cup of tea and we would watch *The Goodies* together like there was never any argument to begin with. I would barely even have registered it as an argument, bending my GI Joe's legs backwards from the hip until his feet touched his ears, because it all happened so often. Adults, allegedly. *Mad.*

Then when Philip moved in, Nana moved out and took Uncle John with her, slamming the door behind them. Philip took up residence like he had always owned the place and he just began choosing what we watched on the television, what we ate and who came to visit. At first, he just felt like an interloper, but that changed soon enough.

*

Mum was thirty-nine when she married for the second time. She was slim, tall, fair-skinned, blue eyed and pretty, with 1970s bottle-blonde hair, teased into a mess of curls and concreted into place with copious quantities of industrial-strength hairspray. She had a fondness for overly short, tight shorts and high heels, and revelled in the gazes this provoked from bricklayers and car mechanics. She was an odd mix of vanity and insecurity, flirty but prone to red-hot blushes of embarrassment. She was protective and capable of enormous affection, the source of warm, enfolding embraces and comforting cuddles. She could also be obstinate, impulsive, reckless, needy, heedless of good advice, proud, spiteful, neurotic, argumentative and self-destructive. She could also be spiteful. Soon after she left my father, Mum fell in the bathtub and gave herself two spectacular black eyes. She revelled in the fact that some of her friends might speculate that perhaps my father had hit her. She gleefully let them think it. Even as she was a victim, Mum could be a perpetrator. All I knew back then was that she was my mum.

My mother embodied a complex personality. There was always something bubbling away inside her. Later in life, she talked about what her life was like when I was about two-and-a-half years old, when she was still with Dad and our tight little family lived in Canberra. Mum said she would leave the unit every day to stretch her legs, her two youngest children sharing a stroller and my brother trotting alongside. She would pause at the front door from where she could see the stove, the iron, and the window overlooking the street. She would check the stove was off – one – then the iron – two – then check that the window was locked – three. 'One two three,' she would mutter rapidly under her breath before closing the door. A little mantra to reassure herself. But it began to consume her. Even when we were older, she couldn't leave our home without muttering those numbers under her breath. One two three. Living with that compulsion could be debilitating, accommodating it in others a daily challenge.

If I fell off my bike and cut my knee, I knew that Mum was the person to go to for kind, soothing words, hugs, tenderly applied antiseptic cream, band aids and a gentle tucking into bed come lights out. But I would also limp into the house knowing that first she would be angry and denounce me as a 'stupid boy', burying her face in her hands shaking with anger and anxiety. It could be very confusing.

Archaeology is not very good at picking up this kind of personality, or much personality at all for that matter. It is a great frustration to the archaeologists who want to inhabit the minds of the subjects of their research. For example, when I scrutinise the images of houses from the Halaf period in Anatolia, some 7500 years ago, I sense a love of 'home' and the security and comfort that homes encapsulate. I see a quaint, pitched roof with gables at each end, a storage jar right outside the front door suggestive of olive oil, water or wine, birds on the roofline indicating food and tranquillity, a little balcony for relaxation and to take in the view, decorative roofing for function and show, and a big shade tree – an oft-repeated motif known to some archaeologists as a 'tree of life', more because it sounds nice than because we have a clue about what the tree actually symbolises.

But if that house was full of argumentative, mixed-up adults and long-suffering children, how would we know? How would undiagnosed mental health disorders manifest themselves in the stratigraphy? Archaeology cannot, for example, provide definitive evidence on whether the matriarch of that Halaf house lived in a state of perpetual fear that she might (*might!*) be allergic to peanuts, consume one in a momentary lapse of concentration, swell up and die. Similarly, archaeology is silent on whether the mother of the household was obsessed with the healing properties of Vitamin C – so obsessed, in fact, that she gave up on the patently inadequate tablets and took to consuming heaped spoonfuls of powdered ascorbic acid dissolved in water every morning and evening for a year until she almost burned a hole in her digestive tract. Archaeology is useless for shedding light on why such a mother might then self-prescribe *more* Vitamin C as the cure for her ailment, a misapprehension only corrected when a chemist pointed out to her that ascorbic acid is … acid. And who knows if there were raised voices in that Halaf house 7500 years ago, gas-lighting, controlling behaviour, threats?

A couple of months after they were married, Philip hit Mum for the first time. During an argument late at night in our cosy loungeroom, deep in suburbia, Philip growled, 'Don't be cheeky' as he leaned over my mother and slapped her hard across the face. Just one open-palmed slap. Imagine the rifle-crack slap as his palm connected with her cheek. The blow knocked Mum to the floor, where she lay stunned – an exclamation mark to end one argument and launch another that would last for the next five years.

The next morning, a peculiar thing: Mum and I crouched over the carpet in the loungeroom looking for blood stains. Mum was falling apart, and I think she was just looking for a little task, a distraction, to get me to be close to her, close enough that she could reach out and hold somebody. Mum's long-fingered hands, which I always remember for the creamy skin and pale blue veins, were trembling. It was dawning on her that she had made a dreadful, awful mistake and that there could be no way back without crushing humiliation. But I was no use. What can a skinny soccer-obsessed ten-year-old do to help a broken mother?

'Come here son,' she said as she scanned the floor for blood stains, 'your eyes are younger than mine.'

*

After school I would walk to Mum's modest dress shop in a suburban shopping mall where I would sit quietly in the afternoons and watch women emerge from changing rooms, smooth down dresses and turn to look back over their shoulders, appraising their own bottoms in the mirror, a pose that for me has ever since been quintessentially female and oddly comforting. Mum was a good salesperson. She would talk her customers into buying outfits through gentle coaxing and persuasion. I can still see her stepping back, resting on one leg, crossing her arms over her chest and clinching the sale by uttering those magic words, 'Hm, oh yes, very slimming.' And I can still see Philip striding into the shop that my mother (and father) had built out of nothing, walking purposefully to the till, opening it and pocketing hundreds of dollars whenever he felt like it. He spent every penny of it on himself.

Like a lot of alcoholics, Philip also had a gambling problem. The money that he took from the till was squandered on beer and horses that never won. And like a lot of conmen, Philip was surprisingly susceptible to the scams of other conmen. One day he declared that he and Mum had bought a new car to replace our sensible Holden. Even as a ten-year-old I knew that we weren't rolling in dough and it troubled me that the new car was a sleek, low to the ground, leather-seated imported Jaguar. I wondered where the money was coming from. To be sure, the Jag looked gorgeous, though a teensy bit out of place in our street dominated by Canberra public servants in shorts, sandals and long socks. However, the real problem was that Philip had bought the Jag from some other shyster and it was basically a gorgeous shell with a decrepit engine under the bonnet, my family sitting in it like the Royal Family, while Mum's money spewed out of the exhaust as blue smoke.

Horses and Jaguars. It was those two things that dominated the first few months of their marriage as we drove to the Canberra racetrack every weekend. I would freeze my nuts off watching dumb horses running around in a big circle while dumb humans bet on them. Mum's money was leaking away as the arguments and fights escalated, and then in December, nine months after Mum and Philip were married, Philip went on a massive bender and disappeared on New Year's Eve. It was 1 January 1980 when he stole that lovely, shitty Jaguar and skedaddled. We didn't see him for days and so finally, in desperation, Mum hired a private detective who earned his money by asking two penetrating questions of deserted wives trying to find their husbands: Does he drink? Where does he like to drink?

They tracked Philip down in Sydney at the Wentworth Hotel, where Mum and the private detective sat in a car on the opposite side of the street, observing Philip come and go with an assortment of hookers. The private detective called in a few favours and two police officers came by to bail Philip up as he left the hotel. With a prostitute on his arm and confronted by the wife he had beaten a few days earlier, he started making threats like any good sociopath would. When Philip threatened to call his solicitor, one of the burly men in blue said wearily, 'You can call bloody Santa Claus for all I care,' and wrenched the car keys out of Philip's hand. He passed them to Mum and the two coppers left. Mum drove home to Canberra.

I was just about to turn eleven when that happened. I recall Mum flopping onto the lounge in tears and so affected by the stress of it all that her fingernails and toenails fell out. Every single one of them.

I clearly remember thinking that another divorce was going to happen. Two in as many years. After all, who could stay married to a man who had hit you in the face, spent all your money, slept with prostitutes and stolen your car? I remember thinking that right up to when Philip moved back into our house a couple of weeks later.

It is not like he returned to a home characterised by marital bliss, however, and he would soon go on another drunken bender and disappear for a couple of weeks, haemorrhaging money in bars and betting shops across the state, his course of destruction mapped against crippling credit card bills. He came wheedling back in due course and Mum took him in again on the grounds that he had agreed to 'see a psychiatrist'. Mum was falling into a dangerous trap, railing against the way she was being treated even as she succumbed to it, a desperate belief that she could cure her violent husband's vices through lots of love, an emotional dependency born of the same desperation, accreted with fear, sadness and humiliation. And all the while Mum's money was seeping away. She was becoming totally and irresistibly reliant on Philip. The more he abused her and her finances, the more he committed her to him.

And so, at a time when her husband was being persuaded to seek professional help for mental health problems, alcoholism, violence against women and erratic behaviour, you would think that Mum would have said to herself: *I really shouldn't sell my old house and buy a new one with this man, and then purchase a couple of racehorses.* You would think that, yes.

This is how we moved into a new home in Batchelor Street, Torrens, and every weekend I found myself visiting 'our horse' stabled near the Canberra racetrack. Our prize thoroughbred was named Moon Prancer, allegedly sired by a race winner of some renown back then, named Sundancer. I remember the stables as stinking, cold places, and the horses as mean, angry beasts with enormous sharp teeth and a tendency to use them. It was all a scam, of course. Stage one of the scam was to convince gullible people to part with their money in exchange for membership in a 'racing syndicate' – they would own shares in the horse and divide any anticipated winnings. The main problem was that the poor horse couldn't run to save its life. So, stage two? Win by cheating.

Bungendore's not such a bad place, although it sounds like a device designed to plug leaks. The small country town is located on the edge of the Australian Capital Territory, a comfortable drive from sleepy Canberra through a rural landscape parched brown during the sweltering summer months but sparkly with frost-tipped grass in winter. People stop there on the way from one place to another, to buy petrol, say, or a cup of tea on its pleasant main street. But meaning no disrespect to Bungendore, a town for which I have the highest regard, it is not the kind of place that people go out of their way to visit, but rather where you might go to see a sick friend or to buy ram semen. Another reason why a person might want to go to Bungendore would be to see a doped-up racehorse run at the Bungendore race meet one Saturday morning. Yes, that would be a sure-fire way to make a quick dollar.

I recall crunching across frosty grass towards the racetrack where a scattered crowd of about a hundred people huddled in small groups with something that fell well short of excitement. It was still quite early in the morning and the shadows were long. I knew the routine well by this time: middle-aged men with little red veins in their noses and overdressed women in too-short dresses got drunk and spent several hours pissing money down the drain, where it was magically reconstituted as a kind of nectar that flowed directly into the BMWs of waiting bookmakers.

At the Bungendore track that morning I was excited. Our horse was going to be running in a real race. *Our horse!* And there were promises of presents if we won the prize money. These offers were made seriously, like there was actually a chance of the thing coming first. Sophie and I found ourselves in prime position near the finishing line, from where we could also see the starting barrier. We watched breathlessly as the strappers led the horses, one at a time, into the stalls. As the race caller announced Moon Prancer over the PA we craned our necks to see. The creature that we had only ever witnessed nonchalantly munching feed in a stall came tearing out from behind the stands like a wild brumby, bucking and twisting, muscles twitching, nostrils flaring, with his strapper holding on for dear life. He tried to drag the horse towards the starting barrier but Moon Prancer was having none of it. The horse lashed out with his hooves, eyes wild and open, mouth gaping. I was naive enough to think this was a good thing. Our horse (*our horse!*) looked for all the world like he was ready for the challenge, literally chomping at the bit, set to launch himself out of the starting barrier and tear the track up, maybe set a new record.

Ah, but if only he would go into the damn stalls. Experienced punters watched impatiently. Two old men next to me regarded the scene with disgust. 'Scratch it,' one of them muttered. 'Shoot the bloody thing,' his mate agreed.

I was horrified. That was our horse (*our horse!*) and just as we were at the point of despair, they dragged him into the stalls and we held our breath. I didn't know it at the time, but Moon Prancer's rangy body was striving to metabolise enough amphetamines to kill an elephant. Yet, as the race was about to start there was still reason for optimism. Moon

Prancer looked skittish, sure, but going into the stalls he had given every indication of vigour, athletic energy and speed. When the gates opened with a loud metallic thunk, several tonnes of horse flesh, all that contained power, exploded onto the track in a blur. All of them, except for Moon Prancer, who casually exited like one of those people who get to the top of an escalator and pause to have a think about what they will do next. Some kind of muscle-memory kicked in a few seconds later and Moon Prancer started to run, but by that time he was a good hundred metres behind the next horse.

The next minute was, to say the least, *very* disappointing. Our horse (*our horse!*) came last by the length of half the racetrack. By the time Moon Prancer crossed the finishing line he was practically walking, the jockey sitting in the saddle like a land baron taking a pleasant ride over his estate. If I recall correctly, the pace was so exacting that he even had time for a little exchange with a woman in the crowd. She called out, 'Where'd you park the car?'

Afterwards, we gathered in the yards where our vet confessed that he may have over-egged the omelette a little. Chagrined, he told us he would watch the dosage next time. Poor Moon Prancer stood in the background, shivering and twitching, the strapper soothing him with soft words and a stroking hand. The horse was sporting a lump in his neck the size of an orange, which our vet admitted was a perplexing development. 'It'll be okay,' he said with a shrug, suggesting that maybe he was losing interest.

Philip stuck with Moon Prancer for one more race, which John and I observed with mounting dread from the stands at the Canberra racetrack, surrounded by the co-owners and a cluster of Philip's no-hoper pals. From where we were standing, we had an excellent view of Moon Prancer strolling across the finishing line in last place and Philip desperately trying to reassure his 'syndicate'. When one furious punter strode up, having bet a fortune on Moon Prancer on Philip's recommendation, I saw Philip put his hand into his pocket, pull out a wad of Mum's cash and thrust it into the man's hands in self-defence. It was excruciating. I looked away. Down below, Moon Prancer was gently reined to a halt by the jockey, and the strapper took him by the bit, walking him back to the stables and from thence to the knackers. Moon Prancer was no more.

Philip consoled himself with gallons of beer and disappeared again for a few weeks on another wild bender. But when I returned from my Grade 6 school camp I came home to find Philip washing up in the kitchen.

'Look who's back,' said Mum with a crazy, nervy, pleading smile and gesturing towards Philip like I should be delighted. My stomach turned. He walked out drying his hands on a tea towel and said hello.

How to explain how quickly we normalised these situations? One morning, a few weeks later, my mother came to my room and told me in a low voice that we were going for a drive. No explanations. Just a drive. She left me alone while she went to John's and Sophie's rooms and told them the same thing. Again, no reason was given, and we didn't ask for one. We just scrambled, snatched up our critical belongings (undies, socks, spare shirts) and crammed them into our school bags, then we all hustled quietly to the car and sat in it, panting as Mum walked out with the keys in her hand, opened the driver's door and took her seat behind the wheel.

Her three children looked to her expectantly. *Where to this time? What has happened? What's the emergency? Was it death threats or a beating?* Mum glanced at her oldest son perched in the passenger's seat with a spare pair of sneakers resting on his lap, and looked again, confused. She asked, 'What the hell are you doing?' Did she laugh? I can't remember. But there was no emergency, we were not fleeing a disaster, running from a maniac bent on violence. We were just going for a drive so that Philip had some quiet time to speak with a friend.

That night we all ate dinner and watched TV together. Normal. To seal the deal, we had acquired a shaggy, happy golden retriever which we named Shandy. We were from the outside the perfect little family. Mum, Dad, kids and doggy. Long-suffering Shandy would patiently follow us around from house to house for the next few years, shunted here and there, sometimes lying on our loungeroom floor having his ears scratched and sometimes in unfamiliar backyards wondering where his loving humans had gotten to, and why they'd abandoned him. Again.

Then, just a few weeks later, in August 1980, we flew from Canberra to Surfers Paradise for a holiday. Mum was full of jokes and laughter, pretending to herself that life was normal and holidays with wife-beaters were normal, and the whole thing was normal, but it wasn't normal. I saw Canberra again just once in the next decade. My school chums disappeared from my life overnight. Never saw the Jag again.

The 'holiday' became a permanent condition. It was a bewildering turn of events.

4. Run to Paradise

Bird motif, Mogollon vessel, American South West,
c1000–1200 CE

Cavill Mall has always been the beating, intoxicated heart of Surfers Paradise. A little to its south, on the Gold Coast Highway, visitors have been able to burn their retinas since 1967 on a bright neon sign of a hoity-toity canine looking down its nose on the tourist crowds – The Pink Poodle motel. It was a name that my mother would utter with reverence and the place was something of a rarity on the shiny-chromed Gold Coast in the 1980s because it was a building that some might even have considered to be 'old'. Today, the otherwise unsentimental people of Surfers Paradise recognise and celebrate its heritage value. Of the sign that is. The original building was knocked down long ago.

When we first arrived on the Gold Coast, Mum would slow the car down so we could admire The Pink Poodle whenever we drove past. She had enjoyed a footloose holiday at the motel as a young woman, before us kids had come along. It seemed to belong to a happier time for her, when she was courted by admirers on the dance floor, played tennis and laughed. I would crane my neck to see this nirvana that Mum harboured such fond memories of, but I always wanted more. A pinker poodle perhaps. All I could see of the single-storey brick-veneer motel, which had an exposed pool out the back, was the tired-looking people working on their basal cell carcinomas in tired-looking deck chairs littered about the barbecue area. But even mediocre places can embody happiness and Mum never tired of telling the story from her youth.

We arrived on the Gold Coast in August 1980, the coldest month in Southeast Queensland, but fresh from the icicles of Canberra we walked around in shorts and t-shirts, our luminescent-white bodies craving the sunshine. It really did feel like paradise. But then, I thought that we were just on holidays. It came as quite a shock to me that I would soon be starting school there.

Back then, the Gold Coast was still being developed. There were dairy farms just a short drive from the tourist strip and little fibro shacks where high-rise buildings now stand. It had an adolescent desire to be liked, plagiarising histories from other places, shamelessly and relentlessly. The Gold Coast has suburbs called Miami and Palm Beach and Mermaid Waters. We didn't know it at the time but it also had a seediness about it, belied by the bright beachy sunlight, the ocean breezes and the towering seaside pine trees.

Mum researched what school to send us to through a rigorous process of asking a taxi driver. In Surfers Paradise, a city full of fly-by-nighters, conmen, charlatans, sex workers and drunks, I was enrolled at Surfers Paradise State School. We moved into a house in Amalfi Drive on the Isle of Capri. It was strategically located a short walk from downtown Surfers Paradise, and everything that it had to offer, good and bad.

Many years later, a Royal Commission would expose police corruption, illegal brothels, casinos and shady bookmakers on the Gold Coast with links to the Sydney underworld. Mum didn't have a clue about any of it. She was a naive country girl, oblivious to the dark undertones, and far too trusting. But Philip knew. We can be sure of that. In no time, he was going into the Surfers Paradise nightclubs late into the night and making acquaintances at the Gold Coast racetrack.

It was on the Isle of Capri in that lovely canal-side house that things really went to shit. Philip got a job selling kitchens and was soon mixing with a bunch of losers, all of them on the take. They would mostly meet at our place for boozy barbecues and sleazy dinner parties. I remember lots of loud talk and raucous laughter with young women in long sexy dresses appearing, disappearing, reappearing and swishing around our loungeroom with a glass of chardonnay in hand.

From the blur of faces and the clinks of empty beer bottles comes a vivid memory of a fellow named Ray, a salesman in his mid-thirties who was transitioning from functioning alcoholic to total disaster. Despite having a doting wife and a two-year-old daughter, Ray became infatuated with a young woman who was an unexplained regular at our parties, breezing in and out in diaphanous dresses, a serene smile on her face. She was pretty in a lip-sticky, blue eye–shadowy kind of way, and I now realise that what I took back then to be a sparkly enigmatic gaze into the middle distance was in fact the glazed expression of a drug user. Her working name was Sky. As an eleven-year-old I watched Ray pad around our house after her like a puppy dog. I watched it all through a chink in my bedroom door, snug in my pyjamas, knowing instinctively that it was all wrong, making my first steps towards devising my own moral code.

Our parties were full of bullshitters of high degree. There was Bill, the South African who told us that he was the President of Australian Mensa, for example. It did beg the obvious question: if you're so smart, why do you live in a one-bedroom unit behind a supermarket and dumpster-dive for discarded meat? And why sell kitchens for a living? NASA not good enough for you? I can still see him boasting of the lions he had killed when he was in South Africa and placing a $5000 bet on him beating the loud-mouthed Croatian in an arm wrestle that never happened, because they were all big talkers with small biceps.

There was tiny Franco Biscotti, a dealer at the illegal casinos on the Gold Coast, who had purposely blown his big toe off with a sand blaster when he worked on a building site so that he could claim workers' compensation. I am not surmising. He would boast about the lousy $8000 it earned him and offer to give us instructions, you know, if we wanted to get some compo too. I was only a child and too timid and polite to say, 'Are you out of your mind?' But it does beg the question: wouldn't it be easier to just get a job and stick with it for a while? Keep all your digits? In fact, the amount of effort that these people went to, just to avoid real work, had to be seen to be believed.

And then there was Reginald, the ageing English painter who could produce portraits and landscapes in oil and water colours, replicating original masterpieces down to the most minute brush stroke. He was a phenomenon. A genius. A prolific talent. A forger, according to uncharitable Mr Interpol, and progenitor of a number of gorgeous paintings that would later feature prominently in our lives. Reginald recalled the 1970s fondly as a time when 'we were churning out the Namatjiras'. He was seriously English-posh, kept alive by a weekly intravenous injection of essential vitamins and minerals paid for by his aristocratic family back in England. He lived without a functioning liver for the couple of years that we knew him (I imagine it as a greenish-coloured mass palpitating meekly in his lower thoracic cavity), but he died of liver failure in the end, a fine painter sinking beers in between Monets.

But it is Ray and Sky who I think of most often, a man demeaning himself and breaking his wife's heart, and a working girl who had other things on her mind. I can still remember the morning when Ray's wife knocked on our door after one of our parties to ask that humiliating and soul-destroying question: 'Have you seen my husband?' We could have pointed to the Ray-sized hole in the hedge that fringed our back verandah, where a drunken Ray had toppled backwards onto our sloping backyard and rolled three metres down the hill. Philip told her that he didn't know where Ray was. It is a sure thing that if he *had* known, he never would have told her. Or it may be that the empty beer cans and plates of unfinished Jatz crackers and cheese on the coffee table were answer enough.

We only lived in that house for two-and-a-half months. It was a blur of bare feet and hot asphalted roads, sea-salty air and sandy beaches, and on sunny afternoons when the tide was out, my siblings and I would scramble across slippery rocks to catch little orange-pincered crabs by the canal that our house backed onto. I was suddenly friendless in a new school and my mother was deliriously happy, or making a good impression of it, embracing the excitement, the sunny climate, the parties, the chatter and jokes. It was a new start for her, away from her ex-husband, the mother that she bickered with incessantly and a host of hungry debtors. Philip drank. He turned yellow and soft with it and his eyes grew colder under their heavy lids.

I have a clear memory of the waterbed Mum and Philip slept in with a bold green velour bedhead. It dominates my recollections of the Isle of Capri. In the afternoons us kids would lay on it and feel the swell sloshing and rocking hypnotically beneath us. And then, one afternoon during an argument, Philip sent us into my brother's bedroom, shut the door, and beat the daylights out of Mum. Right next to that bed.

There were hot-red welts and bruises but no broken bones, so it could have been worse. That is what the archaeology says too. In culture after culture, in locations all over the prehistoric and ancient world, archaeologists find the skeletons of women with fractures to the forearm, a classic defensive injury. Men in all cultures have a long history of physically abusing women – traditional, ancient, medieval, industrial, Stone Age, Space Age and middle age. Imagine a man rounding on a frightened woman who is cowering beneath him, the man striking with his fists, and the woman raising her arm to protect her head and face, taking the blows and the bones fracturing. And that is just the physical abuse – a story for the bones to tell. The skeletons that archaeologists recover yield no data about the violence that *didn't* break bones.

About 1000 years ago, the American Southwest was a thriving mix of peoples, languages, belief systems and art. Those cultures are known to today's archaeologists by exotic labels such as the 'Ancestral Puebloan', 'Hohokam' and 'Mogollon'. Although they differed in many respects, these North American First Peoples were bound together by shared cultural features, including maize agriculture and an array of pottery styles, richly decorated with geometric designs and images of bats, toads, deer, fish and hunched black birds with wings extended. Many of the potters who produced those ceramics will have been women.

*

Archaeologists have studied the remains of many of the inhabitants of the American Southwest to determine what they ate, how they lived, who they were. In the La Plata Valley, a relatively discrete area, a team of researchers has analysed sixty-six skeletons, all females aged between twenty and thirty-eight years old. In the words of the researchers, these women showed signs of having been 'beaten down and worked to the bone'. Six of these stood out as being different – four showed signs of traumatic injuries, all six women had evidence of serious wounds during their lives that had healed, only for them to be injured again. All of them displayed depressed fractures of the skull. The injuries speak of sustained and repeated domestic violence. Injuries like these do not go unnoticed in a small village. People will have seen them – limping women with swollen eyes and tender, bruised muscles – but the onlookers appear not to have intervened, at least not in time to save the women's lives. Unlike the other sixty skeletons, which were found in formal burials with carefully selected objects placed by their sides, these six women were tossed carelessly and unceremoniously into pits. Abused and disposed of.

While there is not a lot of joy in these aspects of prehistory, not everyone was suffering. At that remarkable watershed juncture in time, some 5000 years ago when prehistory morphed into history, when societies began to develop the earliest writing in Sumer and Egypt, and people began to record things, they started with ledgers and contracts and prayers to the gods that they were scared of, but turned quickly to writing songs for their lovers and poems about their children. Ultimately, regardless of race, religion or gender, we all want much the same things for our loved ones – safety, security and the means to ensure freedom from want.

I think of that first slap across my mother's face and of the words of warning uttered by my stepfather, 'Don't be cheeky.' I think of a waterbed with a green velour bedhead.

5. The Good Life

'The Sleeping Lady', Malta, c3000 BCE

The people of prehistoric Malta, from around 3600 BCE, built enormous circular structures out of stone, fifteen metres in diameter, and then they did something inside those structures. We don't know what that was, which is a shame because it must have been *amazing* to warrant the effort that they put into their construction. It's likely the buildings had a religious function. They may have been tombs. They were giant features in an arid and difficult landscape, beaming out messages that we simply cannot decipher. Part of the problem is that we do not know all that much about how prehistoric Maltese people lived. In spite of archaeological excavations going back over a century, we have remarkably little evidence of domestic architecture and surprisingly few intact tombs. It is almost certain that the people were short, a little malnourished and prone to diseases caused by vitamin deficiencies, but we do not know much about what they ate or how they prepared their food, whether they fought for territory or spurned violence as abhorrent behaviour, who or what they worshipped. We cannot be sure how they organised their communities, who the decision-makers were, whether gender or age or some other status mattered. But we do know that they liked fat-bottomed girls. At least that seems to be what the Fat Ladies of Malta are telling us.

There is no doubt these exquisite prehistoric sculptures represent women of sizable proportions – reclining on lounges, resting or sleeping on one side, arms crooked under ample bosoms – narrow-waisted, big-hipped and round-bottomed, their dainty feet poking out from under pleated skirts. To my eye, the message in these figures is not so much sexual (though it may certainly have been) but rather that they are replete, satiated, well fed, free from hunger and want, in a world characterised by periodic deprivation and toil. They are eminently cuddlesome. They represent an ideal that few prehistoric people have ever attained anywhere on earth. They are visual representations of joy.

*

Big-boned females have a long pedigree in prehistoric art. The first Venus figurines appear in the archaeological record in Europe around 35,000 BCE in the Upper Palaeolithic. They are not as shapely as the Fat Ladies of Malta, their waists are thicker, their breasts and buttocks are slack, and many of them boast rolls of fat. Their bodies look well lived in. Venus figurines in this form were a common artistic motif across broad swathes of the European continent, extending from the Atlantic to as far east as Siberia, changing very little in 25,000 years. But what were they? What are they trying to tell us? They are usually interpreted as fertility symbols, and they do look like women who have raised a brood of children. They rarely have faces, sometimes do not even have a head, but commonly boast intimidatingly fulsome vulvas. Might they reflect a matriarchic society? The ladies seem to embody considerable power. If one of them told you to clean your room, you would do it.

If the figures were shaped by men then perhaps they were sculpted to represent sexuality – the equivalent of three-dimensional portable centrefolds? Did lonely men on the Eurasian Steppe furtively pull them out of their bedrolls late in the evening in the Palaeolithic? We will never know. If women fashioned them, then perhaps they represented the every-woman, were affirming and empowering, or maybe even it was women who were the ones who found them sexy?

*

Twenty-five thousand years after the earliest Venus figurine was created, the Seated Woman of Çatalhöyük was crafted in Neolithic Anatolia. Although separated from the Venus figurines of the Palaeolithic by thousands of kilometres and thousands of years, she recalls the same rolls of fat, proudly displays the same drooping breasts, large thighs and dimpled knees. She sits regally erect on a seat adorned with animal heads, and at least one of the statements that she is making appears to be 'don't mess with me'. Whatever she is, the seated woman is well fed, and it is a pretty sure bet that most of the people who gazed upon her were skinny and a bit hungry. No doubt they did so with a hint of envy.

The Venus figurines and their later cousins embody contentedness, probably in a stable home full of food and happy children, a thing that I longed for as a child. I knew this kind of effortless contentment existed from observing my friends, from reading books and from watching movies, but to my younger self it seemed like a fantasy world reserved for the supernaturally fortunate.

On 29 November 1980, just shy of my twelfth birthday, I wrote in my diary: *Soon it will be Christmas. We set up our Christmas tree yesterday. Philip is threatening to kill Mum. Philip said he'd throw her off a cliff. He is really drunk.*

The next day I wrote: *Philip arrived and an argument has erupted. Mum asked, 'What is this, the mafia?' and he said, 'It's worse.' Big arguments. Philip losing his temper. He has a hangover. I have a feeling this arguing will go on all day. He hit Mum. Mum crying.*

Which brings us back to that opulent waterbed in the bedroom of a canal-side house on the Isle of Capri where Mum should have been living her best life. Us kids were sitting behind John's closed bedroom door, powerlessly listening as muffled shouting ebbed and flowed, became shrill and desperate, dissolved into silence. Then a male voice, low and threatening one minute, pathetic and whining the next. Alternately vicious and unctuous. Three kids not knowing what to do.

Eventually, we heard their bedroom door open, then the sound of glasses tinkling in the kitchen and the tap running, then the front door opening, Philip's footsteps crunching in the gravel down the driveway, and our car starting, reversing and disappearing down the street. As the sound faded away our door opened and Mum filled the space, dishevelled and breathless. She said: 'Quick kids. Pack your things.'

I am struggling to find the levity in this part of it. Just three months after leaving Canberra on the say-so of an alcoholic, violent criminal, we scarpered. With nowhere else to go, Mum called an old friend, Joan, who came to pick us up in her little car. Not for the last time I watched as a kindly person was drawn unwillingly into our horror show, trying to disguise her pity, struggling to hide her uneasiness, and torn between the human desires to help but also to flee.

Homeless, we found ourselves in The San Bernardino, a cheap beige-brick motel off the main tourist strip that smelt of stale air freshener. Our accommodation had just the one bedroom, so Mum took that with my sister, sharing a double bed, while John and I slept on a fold-out bed and a single mattress in the main room.

Incredibly, we went to school the next day, leaving Mum alone to reflect in a shitty motel named after some place thousands of miles away across an ocean. An older kid picked a fight with me at school that day and when I went back to the motel in the afternoon, purple bruises were forming on my inside lower lip. As night fell, I remember that there was cricket on the television, which we watched with the sound down low, the vision filling our dark room with flickering light. We ate cheap takeaway for dinner.

Some people are sleek grey sharks. They patrol the shallows with slow, lazy switches of their tails, their every sense honed to identifying vulnerability, attuned to the speck of blood in the water. Sometimes we were what they were after, the burley trailing behind the boat, the shipwreck survivors bobbing in the water, our juicy feet kicking out below the surface.

When Mum checked us into The San Bernardino, in an over-abundance of caution, she had asked the motel manager not to tell anyone we were there, should anybody call. She told him that she had separated from her husband, that she was alone, and scared. The drop of blood in the water. The manager kept finding excuses to knock on our door, which irritated me. He didn't belong. Did we have enough towels? Were we warm enough? Each time, he would stand at the door and look over Mum's shoulder at us children like we were an inconvenience. With nothing else to do, we went to bed in an unfamiliar room that was charcoal black with uncertainty.

After I had fallen asleep, the manager tapped lightly on the door again, a bottle of wine in hand. According to Mum, he said he'd had an unexpected phone call, so she let him in to get the details.

Something woke me. It was voices; a man and a woman. I blinked against a shaft of stark white light on the carpet near my head. Twisting my head on the pillow, I looked across to the room that Mum was sharing with my sister. Sophie lay fast asleep on her side of the double bed, curled up under a sheet. Mum was sitting on the other side, her feet on the floor, her blouse pulled over her head but her arms still in the sleeves. She held it to her bare breasts while the leering shark kneeled behind her on the bed and massaged my mother's pale shoulders, a foot from my sleeping nine-year-old sister. Predator and prey.

But what did that make us, the children? We were not even prey. We were just in the way. I rolled over. I turned my back on it. I closed my eyes against the headlights of the cars raking our room as they pulled in to park. My bruised lip was sore, I was confused and anxious. And I fell asleep.

The next day there were empty wine glasses in Mum's room. We went to school, and while we were away, Mum called Lifeline. Those wonderful people took us under their warm and generous wing. It was not a moment too soon.

*

With barely an item of clothing or a stick of furniture Lifeline helped us move from the Isle of Capri to Paradise Point. Capri. Paradise. You might be forgiven for wondering how bad things could possibly happen in places with names like this, but for us it was like a subtropical *Oliver Twist*. The new unit, far from the glitz of Surfers Paradise, felt like a haven, a place of safety. And secret. A good thing. Rumours filtered back to us that Philip was marauding through the local bars and nightclubs on a wild bender.

We needed our furniture and clothes and school gear, so Lifeline arranged for two big coppers to meet us at the

Isle of Capri home to get our belongings. It was all planned out like the invasion of Normandy. Every detail had been anticipated and a response formulated. Firstly, we had no car, so Mum arranged for Joan to drive us to the house, where we met the police in their marked car down the street because we didn't want to surrender the all-important element of surprise. Secondly, Lifeline arranged a removalist to meet us there, but not just any removalist, they were specialists in domestic violence cases. When they saw us in the street they parked their truck, got out and nonchalantly walked up to us in their singlets – cool as cucumbers, they knew the drill. Thirdly, the police would control the whole situation. They were the experts. They were big. They were wearing uniforms. They had the law on their side and handcuffs if needed. Fourthly, it was agreed by everyone that it was imperative that Philip not be permitted to follow us back to our new *secret* home. That would be very dangerous indeed, as the coppers agreed, nodding seriously. Okay. Got it everyone? Initiate launch codes.

It was mid-morning on a sunny weekday. We walked as a group down the driveway to the front door, all those feet crunching loudly on the gravel dispelling any possible element of surprise, while Mum's unsuspecting friend (portly, forty-year-old mother-of-four Joan) sat in the car and waited, wondering if maybe she hadn't gotten herself into something a lot bigger than she had expected when she'd agreed to give us 'a lift' that morning.

We congregated at the front door and listened. Silence. One of the policemen rapped on the front door and we held our breaths. More silence. Mum put the key in the door and as it opened, we streamed through like marines off the landing craft at Utah beach, our removalist friends in close support. As we hoovered up every piece of clothing, every book, all the furniture, pots, pans and plates, we heard the gravel in the driveway as Philip's car pulled in. The car door slammed, footsteps, then Philip walked in looking like death warmed up, reeking of alcohol. We knew to look at him that he was drunk but it probably wasn't obvious to the policemen who lacked our heightened sensory perception to these things. One policeman told Philip curtly what the situation was and was promptly told to fuck off. Philip was firmly but politely told to step out of the way and was forced to watch us, seething with rage, as we packed garbage bags and suitcases.

The whole thing took about twenty minutes, with Philip standing by the door, alcohol and white-hot anger coursing through his veins. When the last piece of furniture was packed into the truck, we gathered at the front door to watch the policeman sternly warn Philip to go *back* into the house, to *close* the door, and not under any circumstances even to contemplate for a moment trying to follow Mum.

Philip withdrew into the house truculently. He closed the door and we crunched back down the drive. The policemen were first into their car, still in control, just the hint of a strut to their walk. Like the removalists, we were organising ourselves, piling three children into the back of Joan's car, when the police abruptly drove off. They just left. We watched, blinking, as the police car glided past us, braked at the end of the street and disappeared around the corner. Within about two seconds the front door of our house burst open and Philip came racing down the driveway towards us, murder in his eye. Do we cue the comedy music?

As Philip sprinted down the driveway, Mum screamed 'Go Joan! Gooooooo!' and with us all still piling in, Joan floored it in her little two-door Cortina, which is to say we moved gently out of first gear into second as Philip skidded, turned on his heel and ran back up the driveway for his own car. He had it started in no time and reversed out at about 100 kilometres per hour. The removalists, ever the professionals, started the truck and took off too, with Philip hot on our heels.

John, Sophie and I were in the back seat of Joan's car looking out the rear window screaming, 'He's getting closer. Go faster! Faster!' Joan revved the guts out of her struggling Cortina and we managed to pull up at a T-intersection next to the removalist truck, where their professional domestic violence training really came into its own. We turned left. They turned right. And Philip made the chump mistake of following *us*. Our new unit would remain a secret, if only we could get away.

Poor Joan. The day really didn't turn out as she had anticipated. Rather than a pleasant day out with friends, she found herself weaving in and out of traffic with Philip on our rear bumper glowering at us over the steering wheel. We ran amber lights and took the racing line around corners. What we didn't know was that Joan had once been a taxi driver. She knew the back roads and problem intersections, and after a scary ten minutes, we shook Philip off at a set of traffic lights on the Gold Coast Highway. We made our way back to the Paradise Point unit. Our haven. Our safe place. Secret.

Lifeline was not done yet. Their kindness back then seemed inexhaustible. They arranged for a police solicitor to visit us, and with their help Mum applied for an apprehended violence order (AVO) against Philip. The next couple of days were spent watching Mum prepare for a Magistrates Court hearing. There are things from this period that I remember. I remember the police lawyer visiting us in his uniform, carrying an old leather briefcase, helping Mum develop her application for the AVO. I can still see the chairs and table propped against the front door, our paltry efforts to keep Philip at bay after sundown. I can feel my bed under my back even now, against the far wall in the room I shared with John, me reading *Star Wars*, the blue sky out the window and the Death Star behind the gutter up there.

The court appearance went well, I suppose, though not without its quirks. Philip was ordered out of our orbit. Philip was not to call Mum. He was not to visit our house or schools. He was to maintain a distance, of a minimum of 100 metres from Mum at all times. But Philip did not go down without a fight. He pulled the classic stunt typical of abusive husbands who have been caught red-handed. He blamed the victim. In front of the magistrate, and with Mum standing right there listening to his every word, Philip accused her of stealing a ring worth $14,000. He threatened to press charges against the woman he had punched in the face. Mum listened to it all and came home shaken and depressed. 'How could he say such things?' she marvelled.

At least we kids knew for sure it was over now. We were safe in our secret little Paradise Point unit, but even so we didn't take any chances. We still went to sleep every night with our kitchen furniture piled up against the front door.

We were still going to school through all of these events, barely missing a beat. I can't imagine what Mum was doing in the daytime but I can picture her in our silent unit, chain smoking, pacing, crying. I would sit in class and write my English compositions and practise my fractions like all the other kids and then take two buses home with Sophie every afternoon, staring out the window for the hour and a half that it took in each direction.

It was a surreal time, just short of my twelfth birthday, trading marbles with my friends in the schoolyard by day – glassies, cats eyes, tombolas – and listening for unusual sounds outside our unit by night. On weekends, we paddled in the narrow canal behind our block of units while Philip drank himself to oblivion under the blinking neon lights of the bars and dens of Surfers Paradise fifteen kilometres away. I felt that we were working towards something though. Specifically, a life without Philip, a man who I now feared and hated.

*

It took only six weeks for Philip to move back in with us. Mum was very reassuring. It was all going to be okay. Philip had signed up for Alcoholics Anonymous. He had already sat through two counselling sessions with a psychologist. He had, she felt certain, turned over a new leaf. Well, at least we didn't need to stack the furniture against the door anymore. Now the bad guy was inside with us, like in a horror movie. But to me it felt like a betrayal – of Lifeline, the police, the magistrate. Us.

I wrote in my diary that day: *Mum took Philip back again. I don't know why.*

At around this time, I began observing without watching, to look without being seen. I learned how to sense the important things by surreptitiously cocking an ear, to take it all in without raising my eyes from the book in my lap or away from the television screen. I would spend days avoiding eye contact with a man who would exit the bedroom in the late morning and roam about our unit in his undies. I was in the world the way an animal is, calibrating my moods and anxieties by sniffing the air like a dog, picking up the sickly sweet beery-rum scent that Philip perspired after a bender.

I remember Philip's deep voice in the master bedroom and being startled by slamming doors. But I cannot remember what we did that Christmas. Perhaps we went to Joan's house. We have a photo of my mother, John, Sophie and me in a dim room there, on a worn lounge, our faces wan, weary but smiling. I think that was our Christmas that year – tired, scared and faking a smile. It was a long way from la dolce vita.

But if I was worried about living in a unit with a man who had threatened to kill my mother, my brother, my sister and me, and then kill himself, I needn't have worried. Things were devolving quickly. Four weeks later there would be another change.

6. Seeing New Places

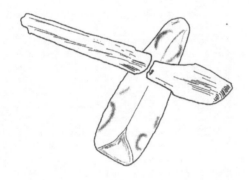

Hafted Neolithic Axe, Britain, 3700–3100 BCE

Sometimes things turn up in the archaeological record that just do not belong. What on earth was the life story of the sub-Saharan African whose skeleton was recovered from Saxon York? How did he cross the Sahara? How did he find himself in drizzly England? The Saxon period wasn't all that long ago though, just a little over 1000 years, give or take. Pliny the Elder tells us about Roman trade for flax from China 2000 years ago, a practice that demanded incredible ocean voyages and camel trains across wilderness and deserts. But even 2000 years isn't really that far back. What about prehistory, before the big ships, before writing, when knowledge of what lay over the horizon was limited to what your father overheard in the next village, or dreamed up?

It is commonly assumed that prehistoric peoples were stay-at-homes, a perception reinforced by the fact that when DNA analysis is done of prehistoric burials in Europe some newspaper will inevitably report that the 4000-year-old skeleton is distantly related to the local bookshop proprietor. In fact, prehistoric people liked to move about, or some did anyway. So it is that we find Neolithic British axe heads, 4000 years old, hundreds of kilometres from the places where they were quarried, some even across a treacherous ocean in Ireland. It is why we find Welsh tin in Germany, traded and transported over sea and land 3600 years ago. These finds say quite clearly that humans have always stood on seashores and on mountain peaks, gazed into the distance, and wondered what lies beyond. Ötzi the Iceman, recovered from the Alps, carried in his cells DNA that is now found only in southern Corsica. His ancestors had made grand journeys. Maybe they did it out of desperation. Maybe they did it because they just loved to ramble. Seeing new places, meeting new people. That is a kind of joy. It isn't always though.

As a child, what I craved was to just stay put. Four weeks after Philip moved in with us at the Paradise Point unit, on a bright hot morning a few days into a new school year, John, Sophie and I got out of our beds like it was any other school day. We made our lunches, put on our uniforms and followed Mum down to the car so that she could drive us to school.

It wasn't until we were in the car that Mum told us the news. We were not going to school. She had bought plane tickets back to Canberra and we were running for our lives: 'But keep your peanut butter sandwiches, kids,' she warned, 'we might need them.'

Philip had been throwing punches again. By this time, we were so accustomed to sudden changes and extraordinary events that we didn't raise any objection. I don't even remember having any questions. If we had to run, then that made sense. I was wearied by it, resigned I suppose, a little upset to be missing the first weeks of a new year at what was still my new school, but I remember being excited that I might be able to see my old school chums again in Canberra. That didn't happen, and I don't remember being upset about that either. I was caught up in the grown-up world and I had learned to slip my thinking into neutral and just roll with it. As we cruised along the coast, heading south for the airport, I watched the blue skies and puffy white clouds, the sparkling Broadwater and the pale-yellow beaches filling with tourists and locals, fun-seekers, happy families, normal people washing off the usual simple cares. We all knew that back in the unit Philip would be waking, scratching his beer belly and stewing on things. That thought was scary and when our plane took off, I recall feeling relief.

At Canberra Airport we paid a taxi driver to take us the fifty kilometres to Captains Flat, a tiny country town full of asbestos-riddled cottages. We skimmed past dry stubbled fields and roo-filled paddocks, as Mum held a pleasant conversation with the driver, who must have wondered why anybody would want to spend so much money on a taxi. Mum laughed it off as a family emergency and we sat silently, knowing by now when to keep our mouths shut because talking is how the best lies come undone. At Captains Flat we paid the driver, gathered our school bags with our peanut butter sandwiches, and knocked on the door of my grandmother's house. I had been here before on childhood visits and knew it as the house where I could hold onto a poo for about three days, just long enough to avoid using the spider-webbed, cold outdoor dunny that 'the jobby man' would empty every Sunday.

My grandmother opened the door with her son – my uncle John – behind her. They were amazed. It was cold inside even at that time of year and we were still wearing our Queensland school uniforms – shorts and a t-shirt – so we huddled on the lounge and ate our sandwiches. We were at least now free from the oppressive weight of expectation, which is the worst part of living with a violent drunk. Knowing it's coming. Not knowing when it's coming. Knowing.

*

Nana was a third generation Irish-Australian and firmly committed to the Catholic Church that she religiously failed to attend. She had a head of wild, dark curly hair, a freckled ruddy complexion and freakishly pronounced bunions. As a young girl, Nana had it tough. Her father died in Belgium in 1917 when she was only five years old, another victim of the Great War, and she spent the first few years of her life in the Redfern slum in Sydney. She first learned how to tell lies when her widowed mother took up with another man, whom she never married, and had three children to him, keeping the new man and the three kids a secret so that she could continue to bank the war widow's pension. Nana was taught to describe her half-brother and two half-sisters as 'cousins in from the country' when strangers knocked at the door.

Nana's skills as an artful dissembler were put to the test when she was twenty and her uncle committed a murder–suicide. He was a shepherd outside Muswellbrook in New South Wales at the time. According to the 1932 newspaper articles, he waited until the property owner went into town one day before knocking on the back door of the homestead and asking the wife if her son could help him with some work down at the dam. He killed the boy there, then returned to the homestead where he beat the mother until he thought he had killed her (actually, the poor woman played dead and survived). He then walked to his shepherd's hut, shot his two dogs, lay on the bed and blew his own brains out.

Understandably, Nana took that little secret to the grave with her. We only found out about it after her death, aged eighty-seven, when a distant relation did the family tree and stumbled across the newspaper articles.

Little wonder that Nana learned how to tell the occasional fib. This was a lesson hard learned and regularly tested. One of Nana's two sisters – Jean – had a son 'out of wedlock' during the Second World War and he lived to old age without anybody telling him who his father was, even though everybody in the family knew except him, and even though he often begged them to. It was my mother who finally cracked and told him when they were both in their sixties! But it was Nana's other sister – Eileen – who tested the cone of silence more than most. Like her sisters, a good Catholic, Eileen fell for a Mr MacDonald and married him in a big church wedding with friends and family in attendance in great numbers. The only thing that made it less than the perfect romantic union was that Mr MacDonald was already married at the time, to somebody else. Eileen and Mr MacDonald were not going to let a little thing like bigamy put them off, or spoil a perfectly good church wedding, so they had a double wedding! While Eileen and Mr MacDonald tied the knot, his *legal* wife married her lover in the same ceremony, changing her surname from MacDonald to McDonald to put the priest off the scent. Isn't that just lovely?

But the biggest lie Nana ever told was that she was five-foot half an inch in height, when really, she was half an inch short of five-foot. That extra inch meant a lot to her, even though she was small enough to sleep in a shoe box. Nevertheless, she was not someone to mess with. She may have played fast and loose with the truth, but she had a wicked temper and a sharp tongue. Off and on, I lived with her for several years as a boy. She helped me with my homework, she Savlon-ed my skinned knees, she made me 'rice pudding' for sweets (boiled rice, condensed milk and cream, with a trickle of honey), and I loved her.

Misery loves company. We stayed with Nana and Uncle John for a few days, shivering in their tiny fibro cottage, wearing grown-up jumpers underneath dressing gowns with the sleeves rolled up over our wrists. Uncle John was unwell, that much was clear. He struggled to walk in a straight line, kind of wobbled and swayed when he stepped outside to collect the mail, cigarette in the corner of his mouth. And Nana was no spring chicken. She was almost seventy and not getting any taller, but we stuck together for protection, the glitz of Surfers Paradise in the far distance. The family brains trust was now activated. The pros and cons were discussed by three adults (my mother, grandmother and uncle) whose shared life trajectories involved bitter acrimony, irreconcilable discord and slamming doors. Only one of the three had attended high school, two of them had been divorced, and none of them had managed to hold down a job for more than about three years.

John, Sophie and I sat on the lounge listening to the hushed discussion, over-sized slippers dangling off the tips of our toes. The adults sat around a formica kitchen table, compulsively smoking cigarettes and sipping tea. Big pro: we were safe. Big con: us kids were missing school and had been wearing the same undies for about four days. A decision was made – we would all fly back to the Gold Coast *together*.

The next day, we all piled into a taxi and made our way back to Canberra Airport. Clearly, it was a time when attitudes towards the wearing of seatbelts and cramming of humans into speeding, moving vehicles were more lax. We flew north, where our unit and clean underpants awaited us. And our car, which we had abandoned days earlier in the carpark at Coolangatta Airport.

Looking back, it was a plan-less plan. We didn't know if Philip was still in the unit, and I wonder what we would have done if he had been. When our car pulled up outside, and when Mum slid the key into the front door, the tension was unbelievable. The door opened onto a quiet and empty space, and we filed in breathlessly, speaking in soft voices, closing the door behind us and locking it. We checked the cupboards and fridge, opened Philip's clothing drawers emptied of their contents. I recall the overflowing ashtrays, sinister with his memory. We marvelled at our good fortune. Philip had cleared out and there was a glimmer of possibility.

It was like that for a few hours, but we hadn't counted on the wicked shadows in the back of Mum's mind that had started flittering as we winged our way back to the Sunshine State that morning. They were mean sprites, mercurial and uncontrollable. They were schemes, longings and desperate hopes founded on quicksand. After a few hours, Mum went into town like a junkie looking for a fix and when she accidentally-on-purpose met Philip in the street outside one of his favourite haunts, he punched her to the ground. She came home barely coherent and shaking. Uncle John's health collapsed with the stress and Mum had to admit him to the hospital. A couple of nights later, Philip came around looking for trouble. Inevitably.

Our unit was on the upper floor of a brick four-pack. At one end of the driveway we could catch whiting and mullet in the sleepy, salty canal, but our balcony had a view of the road, so we could see Philip's car cruise past in the twilight before he saw us. We flicked off the television, checked the lock on the door and lay on the floor to avoid being seen. We waited for the knock. It came. Three short taps, and on the other side of a thin door two breathless women and three children between the ages of nine and fourteen hugged the floor while Philip demanded menacingly to be let in. We lay silently, our anxiety mixing with a sense of the absurd, humiliation and fear for our bedfellows. We could hear him descend the stairs and prowl around the unit, coins and car keys jingling in his pockets. We heard him come upstairs again and knock once more. More silence. More humiliation. Then the jingling receded, a car started and it drove away. Ridiculous. Necessary.

After Philip had left, we lay there on the floor under the weight of the fear and shame for another twenty minutes, then Mum crept to the front window in the growing darkness and peaked over the balcony. His car was gone, sure, but we left the lights turned off, made sandwiches in the dark, speaking in low whispers, and went to bed early, chairs and a dinner table pushed against the front door.

We had nothing to fall back on, no safety net, no backstop. Mum figured that Lifeline wouldn't be in any rush to help us after the fiasco with the apprehended violence order. Same with the police and the courts. Mum had no job, no money, and no husband worth the name, but she had three children to feed and a brother in hospital. Her elderly mother was still with us. Nana made our dinner every night while Mum sat on the lounge, smoking, but I do sometimes wonder how much help she was. With Mum fighting her own inner battles in the loungeroom, Nana would appear shaken from her own bedroom and describe the ghost that she had just seen hover at the end of the hallway then glide backwards into the toilet, just inches above the floor, where it faded and disappeared. I wondered why the disembodied spirit of a long-dead youth should return spectrally from the netherworld to commune with my down-and-out family in a cramped, two-bedroom apartment on the Gold Coast. To use the toilet, evidently.

Nice of Nana to share, but this sort of thing really didn't assist.

A couple of mornings later, Mum made a phone call, and later that day she put Sophie and me in the car and we drove around to a big white house in the quiet streets of suburban Southport. John stayed in the unit with Nana, refusing to budge. The Southport house was set back from the street, separated from the real world by a broad, clipped front lawn and a low wire fence. We were met at the front door by a middle-aged man in dark trousers and a white shirt with an insignia on the chest and shoulders. He was softly spoken and gentle in his manner, and we were told that he was a Major in the Salvation Army. While Sophie and I were sent into a room full of children's toys, he ushered Mum into his office and I saw her lower herself onto a plain, straight-backed dining chair, lean forward with a hand over her eyes, folding herself in half over the handbag in her lap, and disintegrate.

We stayed in the Salvation Army refuge for two surreal and disconnected days and nights. We were not there alone. Battered wives and desperate women came and went, some staying the night in the other rooms. It was a house of hushed voices, sobbing women, uncomprehending toddlers. And then we went home to our unit.

The following Monday I went to school, like it was any other week and like we were just another family. We were fooling almost everyone. Almost. We had been on the Gold Coast for six months. We had seen pink poodles, heard the tinkle of wine glasses and the hubbub of late-night dinner parties and beatings beside a waterbed. There was Ray and

Sky, police, Uncle John and Nana, dining chairs stacked against our front door. There had been running and hiding and running. I think about that sub-Saharan African man that archaeologists identified in Saxon York. I would like to think that he was an adventurous trader inspired by wanderlust and the rich markets of western Europe, who fell in love with a beautiful Saxon woman and chose to make a home with her there. But I doubt it. I suspect his circumstances were grimmer than that. I imagine that there were times when he sat in a poky house in a cold winter in England and thought to himself, 'How the *hell* did I end up here?'

I know that feeling.

For us, after our first stay with the Salvos, it was time to settle down, get into a routine and find some stability. But we were keeping the wrong company for that.

7. The Sins of the Fathers

Detail of Battle Scene, Les Dogues,
Spain, c5000 BCE

Around 2000 years ago, two groups of armed men met in a valley in what is now Alken Enge, Denmark. There was a fierce battle. Germanic tribes faced off against each other, armed with iron swords and spears, protected by oval wooden shields, and one side routed the other. It took an hour? A day? We do not know, but the archaeology demonstrates that after the battle subsided, after the screams of fear, rage and agony were over, hundreds of the fallen were abandoned where they lay, dead bodies exposed on the battlefield, their long bones gnawed by animals, the flesh rotting from their skeletons. Some months later, their families appear to have returned and gathered up what remained of their husbands, fathers, sons and brothers. In what we must assume was a solemn occasion, they placed the bones of around 400 men into a mass grave in a wetland in Jutland. There must have been sorrow, weeping, lamentations. Today, the empty eye sockets stare at us across time, mouths gaping. There is a pelvis with a spear hole through it. Craniums cracked by axes and swords. Wicked slash marks on forearms. Broken ribs.

Prehistory was a violent place. In Spring each year, men would arm themselves, wage wars and glory in the destruction of their enemies. There was horror and sadness, of course, but in the horror and sadness, for the victors there was also joy and triumph. While we might imagine tears at the graves of the defeated, we should also imagine the whoops of jubilation in the camp of the winners. Poems would have been composed to celebrate such slaughter. *The Iliad*, the Greek masterpiece composed in the eighth century BCE, was such a tale, recited by travelling minstrels at banquets for hundreds of years, with descriptions of hand-to-hand combat, of the victors standing proudly over the prone bodies of the fallen and gloating about the widow who would soon learn the news, scratch her cheeks with grief and seek to comfort bereft orphans.

Humans have an evil side, and when Philip reduced a family of cowering women and children to screams and tears, he was tapping into it. The booze was its fuel, a combustible for some fire deep in his DNA. Sober, Philip was a pathological liar and conman. Drunk, he was capable of murder. His capacity for violence was an agitated spirit that inhabited his skin, wriggling and squirming just beneath the surface. Three schooners of beer would bring it out.

Violent men who hold their families in subjugation are at the heart of a vortex. They create chaos. Everything and everyone within their orbit is affected. Truly violent people are aware of it too, and mostly they like it. Philip liked it when the women and children in his life were cowed. That is because, ultimately, it was all about power. Things got pretty bad in the Paradise Point unit after the night that we had flicked off the lights and hid inside. Uncle John's health deteriorated and a couple of weeks later, still in the hospital, he was diagnosed with multiple sclerosis. The poor man grew sicker and could hardly walk but he came home again where my grandmother tried to feed him up and cure him with homespun remedies.

On my twelfth birthday, as I was hoping for a pair of rollerskates, my bed-bound uncle was in the next room sipping soup and gulping vitamin tablets in desperation, while my mother chain-smoked in the loungeroom. I never did get those rollerskates, or anything else for that matter. John, Sophie and I all learned to forget about birthdays. They were a hit and miss affair. A couple of days later, my mother's face swelled up with hives, her eyes reduced to slits, from stress. It was psychosomatic. It was late in the evening on a Sunday, but she put me in the car and we drove off together, Mum squinting through eye-slits, in search of … Vitamin C tablets, much valued, as I have noted, by Mum for their healing properties. I recall stopping at a series of dark and deserted suburban shopping centres where I ran through abandoned plazas looking for an all-night pharmacy. We didn't find any, but if we had Mum would have popped about ten tablets and the 'allergy' would have disappeared. It was all in her head – the illness and the cure. We gave up and went home again, and then she gave up.

Leaving Nana and Uncle John in the Paradise Point unit, Mum and us kids checked back in to the Salvation Army refuge. It was the same big white house in the quiet streets of Southport, the same broad front lawn with the same low fence separating us from the real world, where people worked and saved and husbands didn't beat their wives. We all knew that it was rock bottom. We had brought along our pillowcases filled with spare t-shirts and undies. We were prepared. We'd had lots of practice. We were shown the pantry in the kitchen and the shelf of communal food that we could help ourselves to, and the other shelves filled with tins of baked beans and tubs of peanut butter that other homeless mothers had bought and were not for sharing. I was allocated my bed – the bottom mattress in a bunk bed in a room crowded with four bunk beds.

I woke the first morning to find myself face to face with a six-year-old who I had never seen before. His four brothers and sisters looked at me from the other beds. The sins of the fathers are always visited on the children. At Salvation Army refuges this usually manifests itself in blameless children with behavioural difficulties. That six-year-old was a lovely boy but we could have done without him smearing his faeces on the electricity sockets one afternoon.

Other forlorn mothers and children came and went over the next few weeks, but the six-year-old, his siblings and their mother, and my family, stayed. We ate a lot of meals, for which inexpensive mincemeat was the principal ingredient: spaghetti bolognaise, rissoles, tacos, more rissoles. But we never went hungry. I remember a laundry out the back with an old washing machine in it and an ancient, wicked wringer that looked like it could nip off an errant fingertip in an instant. I remember a backyard that we never played in. I remember a big television in the communal area with buttons for changing the channels instead of a knob that you turned (at the time, something of a novelty). I recall that it was a distinctly female place – there were never any men there, just women and their children – except from time to time, when one of the Salvos visited. And I remember when we first moved into the refuge we had a meeting with the manager, who quietly and gently set out the ground rules. They were not onerous. You can stay as long as you need to, he said, and there are no judgements here. Just two rules: no drugs or alcohol allowed, and no men. No husbands. No wife-beaters. Because lives depended on it.

Through all of this we were still going to school, where I guess we could have told everyone we were living in a refuge for homeless people, living off charity, but who would want to do that? It was humiliating. So we kept shtum, and went home from school each afternoon to a place full of desperate strangers. There was no question, of course, of having schoolmates round to play, and we never visited them either. There was no money for play dates which inevitably involved purchases – lollies, chips, movie tickets – and there was always the risk that friendly mums would offer to drop us home afterwards.

Then, a few weeks after we checked in to the Salvation Army refuge, Mum met Philip in a bar. It cannot have been an accident. It was just another incomprehensible occurrence, orchestrated by Mum who could not pull herself out of the whirlpool. The love that she had felt for Philip, alloyed with loneliness, fear and financial dependency, was becoming an obsession. We begged her not to leave our newfound sanctuary, we implored her not to go into town, but she gathered up her handbag one night and proudly walked out the door. In that bar, which I imagine as noisy and seedy, Mum and Philip got to talking and against the uncomplicated injunctions of the Salvos, Mum invited him back to the refuge. He sauntered in, broad grin, eyes darting – a violent man in a place of refuge for women and children. You should have seen him. Ah, the power. It was a *monstrous* betrayal. I felt nauseous with it and was not placated by Mum's confident predictions that things were about to change.

Philip promised to turn over a new leaf, of course. He was shameless. He got talking to the Salvos and they put him into a program for recovering alcoholics where he found himself in free accommodation with a bed to sleep in whenever he got drunk. It was an altogether excellent arrangement for him. While he was there Philip met Gerhard the German alcoholic. After a couple of weeks, Philip self-diagnosed himself as 'cured' and came home to us, but being comfortable Gerhard stayed for a few more weeks sending postcards enumerating the 'sausages' he was sneaking each day. Quite a few. I can only think that the Salvation Army censors were easily fooled or not paying attention. Ah how Philip laughed. Laughed right up to when Gerhard checked himself out of the rehab centre, came home, had a beer with Philip and attempted to murder him by choking.

But Philip was back in our lives. We all returned to the Paradise Point unit together where the reformed, on-the-wagon Philip promptly got drunk and abused our neighbour from across the road, who had the temerity to shout out late in the night for him to shut up. Philip snatched up the chain that we used to tie up our dog with and paced around our neighbour's fibro home for twenty minutes, whipping the walls with it while the neighbour and his wife cowered in the bedroom. Nana and Uncle John were doing the same thing in one of our bedrooms, out of options.

This is what happens when idiots collide: I went downstairs the next morning to check on Shandy, our happy, gregarious, tail-wagging golden retriever to find that the neighbour had poisoned him. Poor Shandy was lying on his side quivering and whimpering, surrounded by patches of his own diarrhoea. I was horrified. I had seen a lot of bad stuff by then, but I couldn't comprehend how adults could do such a thing. I got Shandy a bowl of water and patted his head, stroked and comforted him, and good old Shandy pulled through while Philip lay in an alcoholic stupor upstairs.

But then a few days later, Philip picked a fight with our sixty-five-year-old landlord who punched Philip so hard in the head that he split his own knuckle. Clearly, Philip was not a man to pin your hopes on. But still Mum stuck with him, falling into a mindset of co-dependency. She became a lonely figure in a forlorn environment that included an elderly mother, a desperately sick brother, and three scared and confused children. The benefit of hindsight gives me little to go on all these years later. There was love there. Mum loved Philip. And there was need. He was the closest thing to a breadwinner that she knew. There was also overwhelming pride. Of the palimpsest of emotions crowding Mum's mind, that pride is the hardest for me to come to terms with. As a child, it felt like cruelty, obstinacy and bloody-mindedness. It is also quite likely that she had an undiagnosed personality disorder lurking in the shadows, which made her incomprehensibly forgiving of her abuser while she became ever more financially and emotionally dependent on him. Growing up, I lacked the language and frameworks to understand that I was being raised by a woman with an untreated mental health disorder.

Meanwhile, the newly returned Philip shared our house again. He used our toilet. He took up space on our lounge. He reduced us children to little mice who rarely left their bedrooms, who slunk about the house quietly, spoke in low voices, dreaded the yawn in the mornings that signified that Philip was awake.

*

Metal detectorists get a bad rap, sometimes because they do not have degrees in archaeology, often because their finds are not properly recorded, and usually because they wear snaggy woollen jumpers and have bad beards with food scraps caught in the whiskers. At least, that is the stereotype. But their work has turned up some extraordinary archaeological material. Misplaced brooches, ornamental hairpins lost by the wayside, daggers sacrificially abandoned in bogs and ponds, and most fascinatingly of all, hoards of jewels, ingots and coins buried under a layer of loam and turf in fields and under oak trees. These little hidey holes are oozing with historical artefacts. Not the grand histories of emperors and earls but, rather, highly personal stories of everyday people like you and me. Every hoard is a time capsule of savings and wealth, in coin or bronze or gold, buried in a hurry by folks anticipating raiders or marauders. More than likely, the person doing the burying was thinking that one day, they would return for it. But they didn't. That is the sad part. Why would somebody *not* return for all their earthly possessions? There is really only one reason why a person doesn't go back to collect a hoard of valuables. They can't.

It is the sadness that comes with this kind of loss that doesn't make it into the prehistoric art. Refuges for battered wives are hard to paint. Homesick children are difficult to render in ochre. Rather, the palpitating thrill of battle gets the spotlight.

Take, for example, the battle scene painted on a cave wall in the Neolithic period at Les Dogues, Spain, around 5000 BCE. Lithe, athletic figures attack from the right, bounding in giant, balletic strides towards an entrenched opposition, men in head-dress desperately defending themselves, out-numbered but trading wicked, death-dealing arrows, their sinuous bodies twisted, the better to draw their bowstrings, to bob and weave. There is bravery and desperation. Was it a silly misunderstanding, a fight over a woman? Or was it humble farmers laying it all on the line to protect their crops (and families) from raiders? Whatever the catalyst, you can hear the shouts and the whistle of the arrows flying through the air.

Archaeologists have found a mass grave of women and children nearby, their bones pitted and splintered by arrows and clubs, enough to demonstrate that these battles were not merely ceremonial or symbolic. They were frantic encounters, breathless with panic and fear, intimate hatred and violence. Clearly though, whoever painted this scene seems to have had a level of respect for the opposition that they, presumably, vanquished. No cowards are depicted. But the fact of the painting says that the painter felt some pride in the battle and its outcome, and his involvement in it. He was happy. The joy of victory.

But where are the children in this painting, the children made fatherless? Where are the mothers, perplexed by the recourse to violence, saddened by the loss of loved ones, powerless and at the whim of angry males? All violence is grubby, whether it is in battle on a Neolithic hillside or in a loungeroom in the suburbs when the kids have gone to bed. But at least the battles described in Homer and on that Neolithic wall are battles between equals. That is the key difference – wife-beaters are bullies who find a sick thrill in abusing people who are physically weaker than they are. They trade off the disparity in power. It is only when the power dynamic shifts that perpetrators of domestic violence lose their balance. Some wife-beaters have stepchildren. Stepchildren grow up and the power shifts. Sometimes.

Living in a house with a violent drunk who had thrown us out many times made me feel very insecure. As a child I learned not to get too comfortable. Just another bedroom. Just another backyard. Just another place to walk home from school to. I became nostalgic about things that I never actually experienced: cheery Christmases, happy birthdays, family dinners. I became homesick for homes that we never really lived in. Houses became spaces that I fell asleep in, passed through, never grew attached to. I didn't invite friends over because I knew that in a few weeks I would be somewhere else, drifting, and they would ask why I kept moving so much and I knew that I wouldn't have an answer that I wanted to give. Or could give. In fact, I didn't even know why myself.

In the end, I left more behind in my childhood than I could ever have taken with me. I left a hoard behind. I never went back for it. It would become the leitmotif of my childhood. When we left Canberra for Surfers Paradise, we also left behind everything that we owned. All of my school gear, old books, favourite t-shirts, soccer trophies, the toys. All gone. And although some of them showed up again many months later, in storage boxes arranged by my grandmother, they eventually found their way into the garage of one of Philip's alcoholic mates and were never seen again. All our primary school notebooks and art class disasters were thrown into a garbage tip by some drunk who we didn't even know. It is little wonder that I became an archaeologist. We fetishise things. And we like prehistoric hoarders who leave in a rush and never come back.

8. Backsliding

*'The Vulture Stone', Göbekli Tepe,
Türkiye, c9500–9000 BCE*

There is something about the Middle East that attracts religions. In fact, strolling down the Street called Straight in Damascus, past mosques, Armenian Christian churches and ruined Roman temples, you get the sense that this is where it all started. And it started pretty weird. For example, what on earth was going on at Göbekli Tepe in what is now eastern Türkiye in the Pre-Pottery Neolithic (some 10,000 to 11,500 years ago)? The eight-hectare tell is covered with enormous, circular stone structures, ten to thirty metres across, equipped with giant T-shaped stone pillars, ornamented with carved mythological beasts, wild animals and insects. The thing is, it isn't supposed to be there. At the time that it was built, people were still foragers, hunting and gathering and coming home to rudimentary dwellings. It is called the *Pre*-Pottery Neolithic because they didn't even have pottery. This was a culture that dealt in wood and stone, and they had little in the way of agriculture. For the most part, what they ate was what they could catch or collect, growing wild. Putting it bluntly, these folks were leading unsophisticated lives, in a technical sense, but they had some complex, multi-dimensional and sophisticated belief systems going on. These beliefs clearly dominated their lives. Unseen gods prompted these people to dedicate scarce resources to building temples to them. Religion, something that humans do very well. It has provided us with solace and comfort – and joy – for millennia.

The first time I went to Syria I had just turned twenty-six. Freshly admitted as a solicitor to practise in the Supreme Court of Queensland and High Court of Australia I made the decision to leave the law and follow my dream of becoming an archaeologist. Back then I had my head in the clouds as I traced my finger over maps and dreamed of Ur. It had taken me two years to save enough for the airfare and I was thrilled as I winged towards the Jordanian coastline from the west over a vibrant blue Mediterranean, bound for exotic Damascus.

As I marvelled that this was Homer's wine dark sea, the expanse that triremes had coursed over, the Middle Sea, the woman next to me – a middle-class, middle-aged American woman – struck up a conversation. She told me she was flying to Jordan where she would engage in missionary work as a Jehovah's Witness. I am not sure why it should be that she had formed the view that it was up to her to fly to the Middle East – a land blessed and beset by every kind of religious belief, faction, schism, dogma. I don't know what made her think that she was improving the country by introducing a religion that believes that exactly 144,000 (not one more and not one less) of the faithful will be resurrected and sent to heaven one day, that those people have been accumulating since Pentecost in 33 CE in some kind of spiritual holding pen, and that Armageddon is coming any minute now and it won't be pretty for most of us because we will all be forever snuffed out when it happens. Our one-sided conversation only ended when we hit some turbulence and the Jehovah's Witness suddenly fell silent, reaching for a sick bag. I left her to her misery and turned to look out the window, a knot of excitement in my belly.

Days later I was sitting on the side of a tell in Jarabulus, Syria gazing at the Euphrates River in the distance and the ancient city of Carchemish just over the border in Türkiye in the north. When ISIS captured Jarabulus some years later, newspapers reported that ISIS soldiers randomly selected fifty men, women and children and shot them all. Yes, that is what Syria needed. More missionaries.

Religion has served the same purpose throughout prehistory. Archaeologists the world over find altars, temples and sacred groves, both modest and grand places of worship, containing little clay models of arms, legs, babies, farm animals. These were votive offerings, symbols of what was ailing (a sore arm or leg) and what was valued (children and oxen), accompanied at the time by vows and ardent promises made to jealous and vexatious gods. What the worshippers were doing was entering into a transaction, a contract with gods who were powerful but also selfish and unreliable, gods that were unpredictable and had to be bought off, placated. If I sacrifice a big enough cow to you, will you please cure my gout? If I sacrifice half my crop of grain to you, will you please not take away from me my gorgeous child who I love more than anything on earth? But the bottom line for all religions is the same. The builders of Stonehenge wanted the same thing as the people who constructed Göbekli Tepe, the Acropolis, the Pantheon, St Peters. They were craving a better place. I sure as hell knew what that feeling was like.

Religion can be comforting in many ways. There can be gods that love, who ask for nothing but pure living and kindness, who bring comfort to the needy. The wonderful people from the Salvation Army were Christians, and their kindness was overwhelming. The refuge brought us the joy of relief and sanctuary, it was charity given with no expectation of reimbursement or even gratitude. It was just given.

*

Having seen our dog poisoned and our landlord crack his knuckle on Philip's thick head, the decision was made to leave Paradise Point and all its paradisey stuff and move to Ferny Avenue, Surfers Paradise, a short walk from the heart of sin-city and all its bars, betting shops and prostitutes. And so, at Ferny Avenue, to everyone's surprise and notwithstanding our proximity to copious quantities of alcohol, illegal casinos and pay-for-view vaginas, Philip and my mother found God. I think that the church, or at least the promise of forgiveness, warmed Mum's damaged heart, a balm that she craved.

For me, aged twelve, I flopped onto the church's doorstep like an exhausted shipwreck survivor on the shore, and the church provided solace and allowed us to feel safe within a community. For Philip, all those generous and trusting people offered an irresistible temptation. They welcomed him like the prodigal son, eager to work God's magic on him.

For the next few months, we were dragged into and out of churches. Strange that the most superficial and hedonistic place in Australia should have so many churches, but the Gold Coast is awash with them, especially happy-clappy ones that call themselves 'Pentecostal'. Born again. On Friday nights Surfers Paradise was a place for drunks, drugs, violence and prostitution, but on Sunday mornings (and during elections) the Gold Coast turned into a po-faced, morally upstanding, middle-class, tut-tutting, finger-wagging community of conservatives. Naturally, our engagement with God didn't involve a dignified Sunday hymn-along in a stolid Anglican or Catholic church. It was more of a weekly descent into madness. Every Sunday morning, and often evenings as well, we would troop with hundreds of other worshippers into converted school halls or basketball courts to sing rousing Pentecostal numbers about Christ loving us, all of it accompanied by spotty teenagers strumming guitars and beating tambourines, at the same time both conflicted and tormented by the hormone-induced thoughts coursing through their adolescent minds. Picture a crowd of people belting out tunes, eyes closed, hands in the air, hips and heads swaying with an evangelical grin.

There were also the healings. At the height of each service

the sick, disabled and maimed would hobble and shuffle up to the stage, full of desperate hope, where the preacher, dog-eared bible open in his hand, would smite the devil in them. Bang! Hands raised in supplication they would fall backwards into the arms of another churchgoer who would be poised behind them like a silly mid-on – 'healed in the name of Christ' – the believer sometimes grimacing just that little bit if they got the theatrical fall wrong. Sad to see them after the show hobbling and shuffling back to their cars, not healed.

And then there was the talking in tongues. People, some of whom could barely speak their own native English, convinced themselves that the Holy Spirit had possessed them and that they could actually speak *another* language. At the height of their ecstatic worship, and in emulation of the believers who on the Day of Pentecost 2000 years ago were possessed by the Holy Spirit and began to speak in divine languages, they would break out in a frenzy of babbling. Some would fall to the floor, overcome. Some would froth at the mouth, writhe and shriek. Then slowly, like a receding tide, the hysteria would ebb and we would be invited to sit and listen to a preacher tell us how we were failing him.

Without a hint of irony, they would push a Christian magazine for women called *Above Rubies* which sang the praises of the female sex while insisting that women needn't finish school or get a job because they should focus on child-rearing. Then there was a lot of reassuring self-justification. For example, we must not be confused by the ambiguity in the New Testament about Jesus driving the moneylenders from the temple. In fact, that whole 'it's easier for a camel to pass through the eye of a needle than for a rich man to enter the kingdom of God' is just a massive misunderstanding. God wants us to be rich. So, dig deep people, and give us your money.

Because that is what happy-clappy religion is all about – making money. Actually, it is about making *tax-free* money. Sure, many of the ordinary people in the congregation are kind-hearted and charitable, but the top-dog preachers rarely are. They are CEOs of a corporation. I sat through countless sermons about how sharing your weekly earnings with the community through taxation is nothing short of communism, notwithstanding Jesus' clear admonition that we should 'render unto Caesar that which is Caesar's'. Yep, tax was a very big no-no to be railed against. Better to give your lolly to the church, yeah?

So why the hell were *we* there, you may well ask? Philip, the consummate conman, was the son of an Anglican minister from India, and knew a good scam when he saw it. He was angling for a cushy position in a Pentecostal church, where the entry requirements are lax compared to the Catholic or Anglican priesthoods. To do this effectively Philip had to shop around. He would drag us with him, a beleaguered family that scrubbed up well, to create an aura of moral rectitude and domesticity. We even spent time in an Italian Pentecostal church where the Sunday sermons and mid-week prayer meetings were all delivered in Italian. We couldn't understand a word of what was being said, but we'd stand in the congregation enthusiastically singing along.

By the end of it I could sing 'The Old Rugged Cross' in an obscure north Italian dialect!

To Philip, the prospect of all that tax-free dosh was intoxicating. Philip cruised through the many congregations every Sunday like an orca on the edge of an ice floe covered by lazy, fat seals. Those congregations didn't suspect the devil in their very midst. And Philip probably would have pulled it off if he hadn't been a drunk. So, it all fell apart. Officially, we became 'backsliders' – converts who had turned away from God and become unbelievers again. Philip probably backslid a bit more than the rest of us, in that we didn't get shit-faced drunk, gamble, beat women and root prostitutes, but backsliding is backsliding however you want to cut it.

The Gold Coast was a place of extraordinary contradictions – alcoholism, working girls, con jobs, praising God and bible readings. Where was a kid to turn? The relationship of sixty-year-old Bernard Willoughby-Howitt and his fifty-five-year-old wife, Penelope, was this contradiction in microcosm. We met the couple at church where the devout Penelope could be seen clasping the holy book to her chest and praying earnestly during sermons with her eyes screwed shut, while the slightly pervy Bernard could be observed sitting beside her, head bowed in prayer, but taking the opportunity to sneak shifty sideways peaks down her wowsery blouse. Penelope had met Bernard in prayer group. She had ventured out of her hermitage in Upper Burringbar in the northern New South Wales hinterland, to sing and pray with good Christians, and in a moment of very poor judgement, fell for Bernard. It was not a match made in heaven.

Penelope once confided in my mother how the wedding night had gone for her. Fifty-five years of closely guarded virginity and arrested emotional development came to a spectacular near-end when the very excited Bernard embraced his new love so ardently that he fractured her sternum. Poor Penelope. I am shaking my head sadly, not laughing. But she could also be feisty. We witnessed one fierce argument between the chaste Penelope and the wild love-maker Bernard. When Penelope told Bernard that he should not be so argumentative, he reminded her that it takes two to tango. In our house in Ferny Avenue, a leisurely stroll from the nightclubs of Surfers Paradise, Penelope stamped her foot, fixed Bernard with a withering eye and said coolly, 'I do not tango! It is worldly, and of the flesh!'

*

For a few months life resembled something halfway normal. In the afternoons we would come home from school and play in the backyard or we would watch *That's Incredible* with Mum and Philip in the evening. I got my report card and was shouted an icy pole. We gathered in front of the television to watch Diana marry Prince Charles in a ceremony that troubled me deeply because Diana said Charles's names in the wrong order during her vows. I went to bed feeling very, very worried that there would be ramifications. The wedding that day was the beginning of a weird, in-her-own-head relationship that my mother forged with Diana, who was another willowy and slightly neurotic blonde wronged by a man. Twenty years later, Mum still had Diana's photo on her telly.

The space shuttle made its first flight. The build-up started when we were in the Salvation Army refuge huddling together with other frightened souls. Abandoned children and battered wives sat in front of the television watching the live crosses to serious American anchor men with perfect American teeth as they talked us through how take-off, orbit and re-entry was going to work. None of it seemed real, although I lived the whole period like I was falling off the edge of the earth, weightless and out of control. By the time we were in the Ferny Avenue house the real thing was playing out. Humans had roared into space in a cloud of white gases and were orbiting my house in Surfers Paradise. One night, as I remember it, the Gold Coast City Council turned off the streetlights and we looked into the black void of space and watched a dot of light streak across the sky. There were humans in that dot's heart. What were they thinking as they scooted kilometres over my rooftop? I couldn't get my head around it. It couldn't be real. People didn't live lives like that. People in my world were victims, not adventurers.

Needless to say, I was lacking positive role models when all this was happening. For example, it was around this time, and for the briefest period, that Philip got a job selling kitchens. Again. Having let down a company called Identity Kitchens he managed to wangle a job with their competitors. It was a little diversionary foray designed to convince a battery of Salvation Army counsellors and a few churchgoers that he was in fact a valuable member of society. It saw me one Saturday morning in a shopping centre where Philip's sole job was to sit politely and enticingly at a display booth and, from time to time, seek to convince people that they needed a new kitchen.

I left Philip to that exacting task and strolled through the shopping centre on my own. At the other end of the mall there was another marketing booth, manned by a gentleman selling sponges. His sponges were second to none, highly absorbent masterpieces. His selling spiel would last several minutes, a dizzying display of space age technology involving a spilled glass of water, a fat yellow sponge placed artfully in the puddle to soak the water up, the sponge being lifted out of the puddle again by a single corner and held between thumb and finger tips (to illustrate the remarkable water retention qualities), and (to the accompaniment of gasps from the five or six people who were so bored that they had paused to watch) the salesman wringing the sponge out again thereby *refilling* the glass with the water. It was spellbinding. The salesman managed to deliver his well-practised patter with a cheery smile. He would then try to sell packets of sponges to uninterested people who didn't really need sponges, at about two dollars each, and then retire to a corner of the mall where he sucked on a cigarette with a kind of angry determination, his lungs absorbing the nicotine like, well, a sponge. He would then throw the butt on the floor, grind it out with the toe of his boot and return to the booth to repeat the exercise, word for word, a hint of desperation in his eye. It was at that time in my life, twelve years old and with the world my oyster, that I decided that I wanted to become a sponge salesman. Philip talked me out of it, but I often wonder what would have become of me if I had been permitted to follow my dreams. Like I say, positive role models.

Our new house in Ferny Avenue was actually an old fibro number and utterly freezing in the winter months. It was demolished long ago but today it would have sat next to the Gold Coast Marriot. The bathroom walls were covered with black wallpaper and imaginative 1970s prints of completely naked women, arching their backs and pointing impossibly erect nipples at me as I soaped myself in the shower. Mum always suspected that the house was a former brothel rented to us by one of Philip's dodgy mates. That would explain the nipples. We lived there with my rapidly declining Uncle John. His sense of balance had failed him as the multiple sclerosis took an ever-tighter hold and he barely left his room. He shed kilograms and chain-smoked. Nana had left us to return to Captains Flat having decided that a lonely existence there was, in fact, preferable to one shared with us in the bonds of familial love.

On weekends, my brother and I would walk down Ferny Avenue to the local canal and spear jellyfish with a broomstick that we stuck a kitchen knife to with duct tape. I made a jigsaw puzzle of an elephant. I read *The Hobbit*. One morning Philip called me into his bedroom to float a money-making scheme with me. We would make kites and sell them in schools: '*Whaddaya think?*'

I don't remember him ever calling me into his bedroom to float the cockamamie scheme of getting an actual real job.

But the Ferny Avenue house is remarkable for one thing: we lived there for a few months, and it was the only residence that I shared with my stepfather in five years that he didn't throw us out of.

9. The Sarcophagus of the Spouses

'The Sarcophagus of the Spouses',
Italy, 580–480 BCE

My mother once read that if you injure your finger, the best form of first aid is to give it a good suck; it keeps the blood circulating to the fingertips. I can't vouch for that piece of advice, but the day Mum accidentally slammed my fingers in the car door in a crowded shopping centre carpark she had them in her mouth in the blink of an eye. My point is, we do things for family that we would not dream of doing for anybody else. We can also be crueller to family than we are to anybody else. Of all the images that I carry with me from this torrid time, the one that has never faded is of my uncle John, a yellow and wasted skeleton writhing in a fevered delirium in a hospital bed on the Gold Coast. It took a few more months for him to get there, though. First, we moved from Ferny Avenue to a new house in Rialto, but this time we did not move into another fibro number decorated with erotic bathroom wallpaper. Oh no. The next stop was a five-bedroom mansion complete with an enormous kitchen, spacious dining room and a backyard that swept down a gentle slope to a glittering waterway where we could fish and fire our air rifle, and play badminton. I was almost thirteen years old, and in case you are wondering, this latest upwardly mobile move was not because the kite business took off. Nope. It was something else entirely.

Once ensconced in the mansion we contacted Nana and she came back up to help care for her ailing son. And so, my mother and stepfather, my brother, sister and I, along with my grandmother and uncle, all lived together in a canal-side mansion for a short time. I can't explain why, but I have no concrete memory of my uncle John being in the house, even though we shared it with him for months. He was a presence and an absence, a low voice in the next room, a flushing toilet late at night. His multiple sclerosis had deteriorated. Bed-bound, he never emerged from his room, a dim space with a human form under the sheets, barely stirring, his single bed pushed up against the far wall. And here is my shame: I never voluntarily went near that bedroom, never once asked him how he was feeling or if he needed anything, because by this time I had lost all interest. It wasn't that I didn't care, instead I resented him.

For the preceding twelve months I had been his reluctant manservant. I had carried him his dinner, bagged his dirty washing, washed his greasy plates and made him countless cups of tea. Lying in his bed twenty-four hours of the day there were times when he would call out, and John, Sophie and I would silently but furiously point at each other whispering, 'It's your turn!' 'No I did it this morning, it's your turn.' As often as not I would walk into his bedroom holding my breath where he would hand me a warm plastic bottle full of dark piss. I would carry it to the bathroom and pour it into the toilet, flushing it and then rinsing the bottle in the sink and taking it back to him, my cheeks burning with resentment.

I was a kid, and I was selfish as kids are, but what made it harder was my uncle's peculiar personality. Looking back, it seems that my uncle may well have had bipolar disorder, although he was never diagnosed as such. Even before the multiple sclerosis diagnosis he was prone to wild schemes, flights of fancy, boastfulness and extraordinary vanity, followed by weeks of seclusion in his bedroom when the mania had passed and his many failings congealed. For example, shortly before Mum met Philip, Uncle John appeared unexpectedly on our doorstep in Canberra and moved in with us for several weeks. He disappeared into the back bedroom and I never saw him. My grandmother brought him his food and drink, washed his clothes and pandered to his needs. In the early hours of the morning when we were all in bed, he would venture out, a quiet ghost who made toast for supper. We would wake to find a plate by the kitchen sink with a smattering of crumbs. Then one day he was gone without a word of goodbye, leaving an empty bedroom rank with cigarette residue.

Family. Everyone who I could consider close family was in that mansion with me at Rialto, but most days I could not wait to get out of there. I looked forward to school, because it was a safe place, a refuge that offered a predictable routine. When I was at school, I didn't have to look at my mother and stepfather, the man who beat her, canoodling on the lounge in front of the telly, Philip with an arm over Mum's shoulder. I guess that is why Mum continued to endure her life with Philip – for her family. Unfortunately, she conceived of her family as including the man who degraded her and her three children. Mum was clinging to a dream of connubial bliss, determined to make it come true by dedicating herself to a tight regime of roast dinners and obeisance.

In Mum's fertile imagination, Philip and her were the man and woman reclining atop the Sarcophagus of the Spouses in the National Etruscan Museum in the Villa Giulia in Rome, a magnificent work of art dating to 580–480 BCE. The sculpture depicts a handsome shirtless man and an elegant long-tressed woman lying side by side on a chaise, his arm draped affectionately over her shoulder as he spoons her for all eternity at a never-ending banquet.

*

The Etruscans were a fascinating people. They sit tantalisingly on the edge of our knowledge of the Italian peninsula at the very beginning of Rome's rise to power. For a time, they dominated Rome, but in 275 BCE, the Romans defeated them in battle and they were eventually intermarried out of existence. They were literate. Or at least some of them were. But they feel like a prehistoric people to me because our translations of the Etruscan language are far from perfect; the Etruscans spoke a pre-Indo-European language unrelated to our own, or Latin or Greek. In fact, they were a mystery even to the ancients. The Romans and Greeks debated where the Etruscan peoples might have originated. Herodotus, writing in the fifth century BCE, was pretty sure that they were the last pocket of survivors from an immigrant group originating in Asia Minor, on the coast of what is now Türkiye. For the past 2500 years scholars have mocked him for it. The Emperor Claudius wrote a twelve-volume history on the Etruscans that might have answered some of our questions but, regrettably, it hasn't survived. More regrettable is that the twelve-volume history of the best sex workers in Rome, written by Suetonius in the second century CE, also hasn't survived.

Recent DNA tests indicate that Herodotus was right. Imagine that: a person who was alive at the time of the Etruscans and who may even have been friends with some of them, knew more about them than academics studying them in the twenty-first century.

The Sarcophagus of the Spouses is striking because it provides a rare snapshot of a reality that was no doubt common in the ancient world, but little reflected in its art. That is, the Etruscans were one of the few ancient societies that celebrated marital love in their art, even sculpting images of themselves onto their lovers' coffins so they could remain bonded forever. In fact, we know the Sarcophagus of the Spouses captures a banquet scene because banquets were a favourite topic of Etruscan wall paintings from the period, husbands and wives sharing the fun. They are far preferable to the ones depicted in Greek and Roman art, which tended to show naked men ogling dancing women and leering at prepubescent boys.

But it was the image of the happily married couple that sustained Mum – the arm over the shoulder, the affectionate spooning, the shared moment, the love seat. In direct contradiction, let me present you with this little vignette: about a year after we had departed the mansion, after Philip had thrown us out yet again, we were living in a tiny unit in Broadbeach. I was sleeping on the lounge at the time. Sophie was sharing a double bed with my mother, which cramped Philip's style and did nothing for my sister's emotional development. Philip was trying to inveigle his way back into our home and our lives, shrugging off the latest beatings and abuse as just one of those things. Through it all we kept going to school, that familiar haven, but in the evenings, with no bed to sleep in, Philip would lie down on the floor next to the bed that Mum and Sophie slept in, like a faithful collie. My poor sister would lie curled up next to Mum feigning sleep and trying to block out the low, hissed whispers of my outraged stepfather, his voice rising from the floor, 'I sleep with you in this bed in the daytime and you make me sleep on the floor at night!'

So much for Etruscan sarcophagi and the warm embrace of a loving and respectful spouse. Instead, Mum got Philip reclining on the sofa late in the evening as the sun dipped in a stunning red sky over our canal, the occasional fish breaking the surface like a little silver torpedo, while Philip, a picture of serenity, would ease back, stretching, scratching and letting rip with incredible window-rattling farts. He would look at you and say with a shrug, 'What!?' if you showed even a *hint* of distaste.

Still, during this brief period Philip actually had a job. At least, that is what he told us. Each morning he would get up and shave, dress in one of his suits and disappear out the door for hours. It was never entirely clear what he was doing but it was always described as 'work'. He would come home at the end of the day with money and sigh, 'There's just not enough hours in the day,' before flopping onto the lounge in exhaustion because work can really take it out of you. And he was still on the wagon. Four months without a drop. There was a sense of something resembling calmness. Certainly, to outsiders, we were a happy family, but it was a veneer that no child of a violent alcoholic is ever fooled by. In fact, a dry alcoholic can be a scarier thing than a drunk one. There was the rising tension as glances were exchanged across the table when the wine was passed around at dinner parties, wondering if he'd take a sip, because that was all that it could take. One sip. Off the wagon. On the road for us.

Another distinctive change during this period was that our house started to fill up with lovely things. Walking past the big oil painting of a matador swishing his cloak across the horns of a tormented bull, or the bush scene signed by the famous Hugh Sawrey, or reading a book next to the cold hard safe that made a mysterious appearance one afternoon, it never occurred to me to wonder where all these items were coming from. Or what was inside the safe, because we sure as hell didn't have any money. As it turns out, Philip didn't have any either. In fact, he did not even have a job.

Still, Mum dedicated herself to being the good wife. I am sure that she had convinced herself that all it would take was endless marital love and home cooking for Philip to give up the drink and stop hitting her. She fed him some quality roast dinners and sponge cakes and the bastard even put on weight while the rest of us listened to the clock ticking away, fretting and waiting for the explosion. People commented on how healthy he looked. It is even possible that his green sclerotic liver was making something of a recovery. Occasionally we would still go to church and happy-clap, and Philip looked like he was taking things seriously. He was certainly gaining something of a reputation for being a good upright citizen, which, as subsequent events would demonstrate, was exactly what he was hoping to demonstrate at that precise time.

He almost pulled it off. Almost. But then, there was Christmas to negotiate, the season of jealousy and bitterness, which almost always saw us in a state of semi-homelessness. Because although Christmas is for family it is also the season for getting paralytic. Families are all well and good, but they really cramp your style if you want to bring hookers home. In early December that year I wrote in my diary: *Today, after days of arguing, Philip ordered us out because Mum didn't want him to drink.* You may recall that the house was occupied by his wife, her three children, her mother and her chronically ill brother, but *he* ordered *us* out!

So, with no other options, we did as we were ordered to do. To stay would have meant bruises and threats of violence.

Poor Uncle John was deposited in a hospital, a man fading before our very eyes, his condition not helped by the turmoil that he was caught up in. The rest of us ended up in a one-bedroom unit in a building called Broadbeach Towers. Great place for a holiday. Shit place for two adults and three children to cram into over the holidays. But we were family, and we were sticking together, dammit.

*

When I was studying the anthropology of ancient Greece, I was taught that there is no such thing as the 'maternal instinct'. Feminist theses were written on it and reputations were made on it. Total garbage of course. Most parents will tell you that they are driven by something deep in their DNA to care for, nurture and love their children. We can be quite sure that in prehistory mothers and fathers adored their children, too, doting on them, spoiling them, making sacrifices for them. They dandled toddlers on their knees and cuddled them off to sleep. Of course, in some cultures, the men were expected to play no role in child-rearing. In others, mothers passed their infants to wet nurses with a shudder of disgust. There were the Spartans, who left their infants exposed out on hillsides to winnow out the weaklings, and the *paterfamilias*, or the head of the Roman household, who was legally empowered to scorn a newborn, consigning them to death or slavery. But there are endless examples of parents adoring their children and those offspring bringing great joy to them.

*

Consider the human figures sculpted onto a bowl from prehistoric Bronze Age Cyprus, about 4000 years ago, that now resides in the Pierides Museum in Larnaca. Around the rim of the vessel, fashioned in clay, the potter has projected his or her ideal life cycle. First, a man and woman arm in arm (what else could it be but love?); then the woman heavily pregnant, her arms either side of a swollen belly; the same woman giving birth, a little head made from a pellet of clay peeking out between the woman's legs, capturing the miracle moment when the child enters the world; then the mother, father and child holding hands – a family, bonded. It is a series of simple and incredibly moving scenes. There can be no better expression of familial joy, a gift to our world from a prehistoric potter who lived four millennia ago.

My mother used to have recurring nightmares about babies. Specifically, newborns. She would share the dreams with us the next morning, craving to share, but the fierce non-communication of her three teenagers, our cringes and squirming, would silence her. You did not need to be Sigmund Freud to know where the nightmares were coming from. That Christmas, Philip did not just throw out his wife, stepchildren, mother-in-law and chronically ill brother-in-law, he also threw out his unborn child. As we checked into Broadbeach Towers with barely more than the clothes on our backs, Mum was pregnant with my half-brother or half-sister.

Leaning out of the window at Broadbeach Towers you could see a sliver of the famous Gold Coast beaches, hear the rumble and pound of the waves, while inside, in the dark, stuffy bedroom, Mum spent days recovering from an abortion, her face buried in a pillow. I do not judge her for it. In fact, without that abortion, I wonder if I ever would have later been able to leave home and go to university.

At a tell in Syria I once excavated a newborn's grave, some 5000 years old. Instead of a coffin, they had used four bricks, about the same size and shape as modern house bricks, to create a rectangular niche some 30 centimetres long and 15 centimetres wide. The infant had been carefully placed within that small cavity and a flat stone placed on top for a lid. It was clearly a tiny human, but the spine, the long bones of the arms and legs, could have been the bones of a bird. The skull was an eggshell, the curved ribs were dry twigs collapsed around the space where her heart had beaten and stopped beating. I gently cleared away the dirt using a brush and my own breath. The entire skeleton fitted into the palm of my hand, all of one mother's hope, all of her apprehension, all of the anticipated joy was reduced to something that was later dug up, sealed in a bag, labelled and put in storage. I found it a terribly sad thing and thought of my half-brother or half-sister.

About 20,000 years ago, in northern Italy's Upper Palaeolithic, in a cave we know as the Grotte des Enfants, two small children were laid to rest, placed side by side, on their backs, as if they were sleeping. The children lie so close to each other that they might have held hands. They were probably siblings. They will have played together in life, shared toys, food and comfort. And their deaths almost certainly occasioned bitter grief and lamentations. Somebody – presumably family – scattered hundreds of seashells about their bodies, a kind gesture that even at the time must have felt paltry and insufficient. We should envision the sad gathering around the small grave in a cool damp cave, but we must not forget the squeals and toddler-talk evoking smiles and happiness, bouncing off the walls and echoing through that cave some twenty millennia ago. Or the burial of a mother and her infant interred together 6500 years ago in the Scandinavian Mesolithic on the island of Vedbaek, the coupling of mother and child, the most powerful of bonds, commemorated in a scattering of red ochre, the teeth of a red deer and wild pig strung as a necklace or head covering. These finds represent powerful bonds, the emotions of parenthood. They are symbolic of the pure unadulterated goodness of family, that can be poisoned by a selfish man who drinks too much and places his own gratification through alcohol above all other things and throws punches when he is drunk.

After about three weeks, we moved out of Broadbeach Towers. With the help of a local church, we moved into a unit in Mermaid Waters. Broad beaches. Waters full of mermaids. It all sounds so lovely, but we did not even have the money for a fridge. We kept our milk cool in a sink full of water. I couldn't bear the tepid stuff, skipped my breakfasts, and fainted leaving Kmart one day.

Uncle John, who had been admitted to hospital, moved back in with us after he was discharged – his balance gone, his confidence shot, his will broken. With two of us supporting him under each arm, he weaved and staggered into his room and flopped onto the bed where he was soon marooned. He never really came out again.

With hardly any clothes, we bided our time and one morning waited outside the old mansion. When Philip left the house we ran inside and scooped up the belongings we could carry, threw them into the car and drove back like lords to our new apartment. We spent a sad Christmas there listening to a Beach Boys cassette that my brother had received as a gift.

I had the sense that we had reached a tipping point and that even Mum had finally worked out how futile it was to pin any hopes on Philip. She sat by herself at the dining table in the mornings, deep in thought, sipping milky tea and smoking. That New Year's Eve, we babysat for a woman, Jenny, who we had met in the Salvation Army refuge. We all trooped around to Jenny's house in the afternoon and while I played with her kids, Jenny dolled herself up for a night on the town with friends. There were eight children in the house that night with Mum in one of the bedrooms, gazing into the darkness, contemplating the year ahead, dwelling on the child she had lost. In the morning, she asked us what we thought about the electric organ playing during the night. We said we hadn't heard anything. It wasn't actual music, she explained, just toneless noises, loud and discordant, random notes, like someone was thumping the keys. We suggested it might have been one of Jenny's children, but Mum corrected us. She had gotten up in the middle of the night to check, she told us, and even though she could see the room was empty she could still hear the notes. She claimed it was a ghost. We could say nothing to help her. She was hearing her own ugly music.

I was just about to turn thirteen and still thought of adults as being wiser by virtue of their age and experience, but I was quickly working out, way too young, that the world is full of flawed human beings who you really should not rely on. John, Sophie and I just learned to roll with the punches, surrendering to the fact that we were, for a little longer, powerless in a wild storm. When the storm passed, we would come out from our hidey-holes. When the wind started again, we would hunker. In the meantime, we just quietly accepted that our mother was hearing tone-deaf ghosts bashing out show tunes on New Year's Eve.

Of course, a couple of weeks later, inevitably, Mum and Philip 'reconciled', which is what the church called it. At the time, my brother, John, was washing dishes for one of the pastors from the church who owned a restaurant on the tourist strip. John recalls the evangelical preacher walking into work and booming loudly: 'Good news. Your parents are back together!' The church certainly put a high price on 'saving a marriage'. And so we moved back into that big mansion full of collectible oil paintings and a safe full of ill-defined valuables, while Nana and Uncle John stayed in the Mermaid Waters unit. They'd had enough and who could blame them. They were, after all, family.

Just a few weeks later, Mum took a call from the Gold Coast Hospital. Uncle John was sick. He was very sick. And then, just like that, he was dying. Mum must have considered that we needed 'closure', so we parked in the carpark of the Gold Coast Hospital and walked as a group to the elevators. I remember Philip, in a rare moment of common sense, asking Mum if she was sure we should see Uncle John 'like that' and Mum holding her ground. 'They need to see it,' she said determinedly. We exited the lift and walked to a ward with an expansive view of the Southport Broadwater. It was gorgeous, blue and sparkly, a bright clear day. The horizon razor-sharp. They took us to Uncle John's bed across squeaky hospital floors (all normal so far) but when we got to the edge of his bed I felt the blood drain from my cheeks. Where was my uncle? He had withered to the size of a child. His grown man's body had been reduced to a shadow. He was a skeleton embalmed in tight pale skin, his eyes closed under parchment eyelids, sunk deep into his skull. He was delirious, moaning softly, working his mouth, sliding towards his final coma, dying of septicaemia.

After we had moved out of the Mermaid Waters unit, Nana had done her best to look after her son. Alone, growing old herself, she had given him sponge baths in his bed because neither of them had the strength to get him to the shower. She had fed him Vitamin C, made his porridge, grilled his chops, but unable to leave his bed and lacking the strength to roll from one side of his body to the other, he had developed bed sores and then blood poisoning. That day in the hospital I stared at my uncle, a child-man in hospital nappies curled into the foetal position. I was aghast. Uncle John and I shared a visceral bond: I had brushed and rinsed his false teeth, I had emptied his piss bottle. When watching his suffering became unbearable we left in silence. He died later that day.

My mother told me many years later that a few weeks before his death she had sat with Uncle John and they had talked about how their lives were panning out. Reflecting on her own dismal circumstances, Mum had confided in her brother, 'I wish I had never been born.'

'Oh no, I don't!' Uncle John had replied emphatically. 'I've had a great life.'

10. Shiny New Things

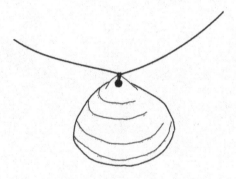

Shell necklace, Cyprus, c1750 BCE

Some people enthusiastically embrace new technology. For example, I remember when email was first introduced to the workplace. I was working in a law firm and one of the solicitors, who was quick to grasp the full potential of the medium, sent a sneaky email from another solicitor's computer to a secretary that read: *Come into my office if you want to know why they call me Russell the Love Muscle.* Poor Russell. A lovely fellow. Married with two small children. The perpetrator was never caught (it wasn't me) but it took just forty-eight hours from the introduction of the most powerful communication tool in the history of humankind to the first inappropriate email. Frankly, I'm amazed it took that long.

But things go in and out of fashion and sometimes it is hard to know why. Sometimes it only takes a few years, while other iconic fashions last for centuries. On Chalcolithic Cyprus, for example, they made pretty much the same pottery for 1500 years between 3900 and 2400 BCE. Then, all of a sudden (in archaeological terms), radically new shapes, colours and decorative techniques appeared. Enter the prehistoric Bronze Age where, you guessed it, they made pretty much the same pottery for another 700 years. Then suddenly everything changed again. Archaeologists love this stuff. Was each change caused by an invasion? Was it a change from within, and if so, why? Maybe it isn't all that complicated. After all, you would think that after 700 years people would be about ready for a different coloured pot.

Fashions may come and go but humans typically love new things. Especially, they love shiny new things. Furthermore, they are always on the lookout for ways of getting those things that little bit cheaper. A good conman like Philip was hyper-aware of this fact. Also, a good conman appreciates that you have to wear nice stuff and live in a fancy house because looks can be deceiving and for a conman, deceit is everything.

One of the frustrating aspects of my relationship with Philip was that some of my school friends actually thought we were rich. After all, we sometimes lived in big houses and drove foreign cars. My friends never saw the empty fridges, they never saw Philip starting the Jaguar with a screwdriver because the ignition had fallen out, and they weren't around when the cars got repossessed or the landlord sent big men around to threaten us for not paying the rent. But you need the nice house and fancy car because a mark is more likely to part with their money to a conman who looks rich rather than to some loser with his arse out the back of his trousers.

And so, Uncle John died in the middle of a humid Gold Coast February and we went home to a mansion. I still feel bad about what happened but cannot begin to imagine the weight of the guilt that must have settled on Mum's shoulders. Poor Uncle John passed out of our lives in the same way that he used to move on from one of his 'episodes', leaving early one morning, a plate on the sink smattered with toast crumbs, not saying a proper goodbye.

Nana's brother – Uncle Dolph – came to visit with his wife, Hazel, to express his condolences. Like Nana, Uncle Dolph had a tough upbringing. At the start of World War II he signed up with his brother Warwick and the two lads shipped off to Singapore together. In Dolph's case, he left a fiancée behind and was additionally handicapped with the unfortunate Christian name of Adolphus! I mean, what if he'd ended up in the company of the French resistance? During the Fall of Singapore, the two brothers were captured by the Japanese, transited through Changi, and ended up prisoners-of-war in Japan, digging coal near Fukuoka. Dolph watched his brother die of malnutrition in the final weeks of the war. While he languished in the POW camp, Dolph's Protestant fiancée visited his Catholic mother's home every morning asking for news of her lover. Every morning she was told the same thing – he was still listed as 'missing in action' – even long after the family had been advised that he was not missing but actually a *living* POW.

Inevitably, predictably, Dolph came home to find that his fiancée had lost hope, given up on him, and was living in Arkansas with her American fly-boy husband. Undaunted,

Dolph had the pertinacity to fall in love with another Protestant, Hazel, whom he married. The poor woman spent the rest of her life being judged by her husband's Catholic family as being morally inferior. This was a Catholic family that, we must recall, was characterised by adultery, illegitimate children, a murder–suicide and bigamy. Hazel tried hard but she never stood a chance. For example, when the neighbour's dog bit her and had to be put down, uncompromising Auntie Jean said that they should have shot Hazel and kept the dog.

In some kind of karmic payback, however, when he was in his sixties, Uncle Dolph won the lottery. I remember my mother being delighted for him. Philip was too. Absolutely delighted. That was part of the reason that Uncle Dolph had come to visit, of course. He was passing on his condolences, sure, but when Mum and Philip invited him over for afternoon tea in the loungeroom of our fraud of a mansion, Philip asked Uncle Dolph if he was interested in investing in a great opportunity that he had going, a sure thing. Wisely, Uncle Dolph declined. I remember overhearing the conversation as Philip poured cups of tea and Mum doled out the scones and cream. I was horrified and felt the sting of shame. For the first time, that shame extended to my mother who was changing before my eyes. I had been raised on stories of Uncle Dolph surviving on tiny bowls of rice and gruel through the war. In old age, he dodged another bullet and that bullet was my stepfather, my mother sitting beside him demurely. It was a baffling and demoralising low point, and proof – if proof were needed – that poverty, insecurity and dependency can make wretches of us all.

The mansion on the canal was the perfect stage for what was next to come. Oil paintings, silverware, exotic time pieces and vases of Venetian glass continued to mysteriously appear. Nana was back living with us, recovering from the death of her son. I do not remember her passing any comment on the collectibles hanging on our walls and resting on the mantlepiece, nor do I remember any of us being especially surprised when Philip announced that he was shouting us all a holiday on expensive Hayman Island. We had all lived through so much bizarro-world shit by then that an unaffordable holiday barely registered.

In April, with the weather cooling, less than two months after the death of Uncle John, we all clambered into the car and struck out for north Queensland – Mum and Philip in the front, Nana, John, Sophie and I crammed into the back seat.

It is a long way from the Gold Coast to the Whitsundays. It is certainly a long way to drive, twelve hours in fact, so a sensible decision was made to break it up by staying overnight in a motel at the halfway mark. I do remember thinking that it was weird as we pulled into a random motel off the highway at Caloundra after only two-and-a-half hours on the road. We spent the better part of the day, and the day after that, just sitting around. Well, we didn't *all* just sit around. Philip disappeared for a while. John, Sophie and I were completely mystified and hugely frustrated, three Gold Coast kids stalled in Caloundra, which in our view was just a poor imitation of the Gold Coast. I fell asleep on the second night with no Philip in the room but when I awoke the next morning, he was lying asleep in the bed next to Mum. Odd. We all got up, ate breakfast and hit the road, this time making it all the way up the coast.

We had a ball on Hayman Island. After a few torrid years it felt like a genuine holiday, like we really were leaving our problems behind. We swam in the pool, took part in an archery competition, sang along with the in-house entertainer each evening and played billiards. We met some lovely people who thought of us as fellow cashed-up globetrotters, and we also met a very big man with a smudged tattoo who seemed to be travelling on his own and who looked like he would be more at home in a small-town betting shop than at a five-star island resort. He would sit on a bar stool drinking beer, intently watching John, Sophie and me as we played table tennis and shuttlecock. He asked us our names. He asked where we were from. He didn't smile. He creeped us out so much that we told Mum and Philip, which saw Philip anxiously demanding a full description and disappearing into the night to find him. It seemed like an odd time for Philip to suddenly start getting protective of us. I remember Philip coming back to our room about twenty minutes later, telling us he had found the man, had had a word, sorted everything. He must have. We didn't see the bloke again.

Mostly my grandmother wouldn't leave the cabin because she had read that coconuts can fall on peoples' heads and kill them. At dinner time we would weave and bob between coconut trees to the restaurant, always alert to the dire possibilities. As it turns out, having our skulls crushed like a coconut by a coconut was the least of our worries; back in our mansion on the Gold Coast some good-for-nothings were breaking into our lovely big canal-side home and were stealing all those remarkable paintings. What is more, they had cut through the safe with an oxyacetylene torch and had stolen everything inside (it was fully loaded up with diamond jewellery and silverware, as it turns out). When Philip found out we had been robbed he rushed back home like any good citizen would. There were police reports to make. All those gorgeous paintings! The Murano glass! The diamonds! Boy, lucky we were insured.

Fake masterpieces have a price. Safes cost money, too, even when they are empty. Big mansions on Gold Coast canals are not cheap things to rent either. And insurance policies do not grow on trees. All of these things are expensive, and my flatulent, alcoholic stepfather had no visible means of support. But what he had was a posh English accent, a family that made him look respectable and an alcohol-abuse problem that rendered him incapable of saying no to quick cash and hare-brained schemes, no matter what the risks involved or how dubious the company it required him to keep. My stepfather never could have come up with a scam so elaborate as the 'Big Burglary', although it was rumoured that he was once on Interpol's most wanted list for selling Tangalooma Island to a cousin of the Queen. That was before we met him. By the time he had cosied up to us, Philip was strictly a low-rent conman who was raising his sights beyond his abilities when he peddled vibrating therapeutic equipment to arthritic pensioners in need of pain relief (he sold the same vibrating therapeutic equipment to thirty-five-year-old married pre-internet couples who were also in need of relief but too embarrassed to purchase sex toys). True that!

So, where *did* those paintings, jewels and vases come from? Firstly, most of them never existed. The safe was empty and the paintings were forgeries. All those things, and the rent on the house itself, were paid for by a Gold Coast criminal named Normie. I only ever met Normie a few times. He seemed like an okay bloke, one of those gruff middle-aged men who would give a young lad a wink, but he was hard, and he didn't speak much. He had the look of a former rugby league player about him, the kind that might have had a career cut short by an unsavoury eye-gouging incident. Normie was always in the company of a hanger-on, another big bloke, usually with fading tattoos. Being Gold Coast crims (as opposed to the more stylish Melbourne variety) they typically wore snug shorts and rubber thongs. Normie was not somebody to mess with. He was an old mate of career criminal Lenny McPherson, the notorious Sydney underworld figure, known for gambling, prostitution and decades of violence. Normie could barely disguise the contempt that he held Philip in, which Philip must have picked up on and which made him nervous. It was widely reported that some of Normie's former colleagues had mysteriously disappeared. Whether that was true or not, he scared the shit out of us kids, and Philip was petrified of him. After all, Normie had shelled out thousands of dollars to set the whole scam up. He had invested heavily in the crime and could potentially lose his money. If Philip was arrested and got mouthy then Normie was in serious strife too. Philip was his patsy and from the moment the burglary was reported to the police, Philip was also his obedient, fearful servant.

Still, I owe Normie for a wonderful holiday on exclusive Hayman Island. Yep. Normie paid for that too.

*

When we returned from Hayman Island, after the burglary had been reported to the police and the insurance claim had been made, it was clearly a good time for Philip to lie low. Naturally, the idea now was to just stay cool, attract as little unwanted attention as possible, and at all costs, avoid any entanglements with the police. After all, Philip and Normie and his pals had come too far to fuck it all up now. Drawing inspiration from months of meticulous planning and appreciating the imperative to keep his head down, Philip took Mum out to dinner eight days after our return from Hayman Island, got drunk, and beat her up. Well, why not? It was their wedding anniversary.

I wrote in my diary: *Last night Philip got drunk. I think he hit Mum. Lots and lots of arguing. I think it's about separation time.*

All these years later, it is the insouciance of the diary entry that strikes me. Drunk stepfather. Beaten mother. The weary resignation in the face of dislocation and mayhem. In spite of my prediction, inured to it all by now, or just plain out of energy or options, Mum stuck around and we waited anxiously for the binge to dissipate. Philip stayed drunk for days, sobered up a little, then spent the next six weeks inviting a seemingly endless procession of strangers and vague acquaintances over to our place for barbecues. Of course, the barbecues were just a cover, an excuse for downing huge quantities of beer. Given the grim circumstances and his wife's lingering sorrow (remember, it was only a couple of months since her brother had died and a few months since the abortion), Philip looked deep into his heart and found nothing within himself except the desire to get shitfaced.

In the weeks following the Big Burglary Philip grew unhinged. His eyes turned a jaundice yellow, but still he kept drinking, the alcohol and the toxins feeding the inexplicable rage swelling like a tumour inside him, a rage that had no target and no reason. We would slink from our bedrooms to the kitchen, avoid eye contact, interaction, conversation. Avoid *him*. He became a knot in our bellies, a darkness on the edge of a sunny day, an eclipse without the awe.

Children on the Gold Coast back then went barefoot. We would walk to school without shoes, we all had soles toughened by melting asphalt and baking concrete footpaths, and every kid grew up knowing what a patch of bindi-eye looked like. We were ever alert to it, knew exactly when to stop at the first sting of the prickles, to stand on one foot and pull the tiny thorns out and back away again carefully. Philip was like that. A patch of bindies that you were alert to, skirted and sometimes got hurt on.

I wrote in my diary: *Philip is really bad this time. He is very sick from the drink and is in very deep with the mob. They will knock him off or give him to the police as soon as they're finished with him.*

And in the middle of all that, one of Mum's creditors, one of the people owed money by that little dress shop in Canberra that Mum had built out of nothing and which Philip had stripped of every penny, had Mum declared bankrupt. Philip didn't seem to care. In fact, it suited him because this made Mum even more dependent on him. The humiliation for Mum must have been all but insupportable.

Talk about post-holiday blues.

*

Although he was a bum, Philip had always enjoyed the finer things in life. In particular, he liked a smart suit. He always had two or three of them in his wardrobe and when it was time to fleece some poor sucker, he would take one out of the closet, put it on and sally forth, vibrating therapeutic equipment in hand. His suits were tools of the trade. After weeks of binge drinking, slamming of doors, breaking beer glasses, crying, shrieks, slaps, screaming and foreboding silence, it all came to a head.

Of course, Mum was acutely aware that the physical safety of her children depended on her placating Philip, so she stoked up the barbecue one night and set fire to every stitch of clothing in his wardrobe. Infantile, yes. Satisfying, I suppose. Stupid, undoubtedly.

It rolled on for a couple more weeks and somewhere in there Philip laced his yellow sausage-fingers around Mum's

Nefertiti throat and squeezed until she passed out. And then, remarkably, and for the only time ever, Philip moved out, leaving us in the house. A discombobulating departure from the established norm which would usually have seen us thrown out on our arses. But we soon learned it wasn't due to Philip's kindness or generosity. Word had made it through to Normie, and Normie was not happy. Normie told Philip to dry out. Like a timid little puppy, Philip did as he was told.

Taking a look around the mansion, little clouds of fingerprint dust still sitting on some of the smoother surfaces, Mum might have considered this a stroke of luck, an incredible opportunity. She might have thought to herself, 'Let's get away, a long way away.' She didn't though. Instead, about three weeks later, Philip reappeared on our front doorstep, a little less yellow, hands shaking for want of a drink, and begging for forgiveness.

In my diary I wrote: *Mum took him back.* And then: *We needed money. Only thing left to do.*

And all of it was about the pursuit of glittering new things. If it hadn't been for the way that Philip and Normie craved easy money, and the way that people value shiny baubles, none of it ever would have happened. But humans love those shiny baubles. They bring us joy. Archaeologists find them all over the prehistoric world. Sometimes the baubles are not exactly what we would classify as amazing stuff today, but times were simpler then, so (for example) we find humble seashells transported several days on foot from the ocean, traded inland and perforated for taking a thread, so that they could be worn as a necklace. I have found a few of them myself and always imagine the woman (of course, it may have been a man) strutting around her prehistoric village with her new bling, a simple seashell necklace. It is touching because it *was* simple but valued.

I also think of the ancient Sumerian poem that I distantly recall reading as a young student, written by a lover for her man, describing him as her 'celery beside still water'. Celery? Pretty basic. A vegetable product but something that hungry people rather liked.

Poor people like baubles too, of course, and they have always been willing to go to great lengths to acquire them. That is why good archaeologists are alert to the fact that the pretty things that they find may have a complicated pedigree. I often watch *Antiques Roadshow* and think to myself 'Yeah, sure!' when the proud owners of an antique silver hairbrush describe it as 'a gift to great Aunty Mabel who was a maid to Lady Prestwick of the manor'. Sticky fingered Aunty Mabel, eh? But we have enough wonderful artefacts recovered from places characterised by poverty to know that people struggling to get by also derived great pleasure from lovely things. That is why archaeologists sometimes find the most exquisite pieces of art in places where leisure time might have been better spent planting seeds or hunting for meat. We must consider the craftsperson, tummy rumbling with hunger, going the extra mile to create something beautiful, knowing that its very beauty would bring them or their loved one joy.

That is why, from time to time in Ireland, archaeologists turn up jadeite polished axe heads from the Neolithic. There are four in the Irish National Museum, one that is twenty-seven centimetres long and nine centimetres wide. It is a sleek, speckled-green beauty that would have taken some 100 hours to shape, grind and polish in about 4000 BCE. Jadeite is a very hard stone, excellent for axe heads, but there are other kinds of rock in Ireland that are hard and good for axe heads. So, why jadeite? Well. The thing about the jadeite used to make those Irish pieces, around 6000 years ago, is that it came all the way from the Italian Alps, from a quarry 2000 metres up, accessible only in the warmer months. Why go to so much trouble when there were good local options that could have been used instead, and also could have been sourced without the risk of plummeting to one's death! The jadeite had to be pulled out of the earth, hauled down a steep mountain or two, and transported 2000 kilometres to Ireland, including across a stretch of the Atlantic Ocean! How many middlemen were there? What was exchanged for the jadeite? And how on earth did some person in Ireland even know about the Italian quarry in the first place? It is a hell of a lot of effort for a piece of greenish rock. I mean, jadeite axes look nice, but not *that* nice! Clearly, this was a bauble. It had value, maybe as a sacred object and certainly as a status symbol. But mostly, I think, owning it simply brought the owner joy. We can imagine him running his fingers along the edge affectionately, turning it over in his hand, showing it off to his mates smugly: 'Do you like me axe? Yeah … It's Italian.'

The mansion was a bauble. It glittered and distracted. The forged paintings and make-believe contents of the safe were baubles. They attracted an insurance company and the premiums where its profits lay. The insurance payout was a bauble. An irresistible lure for Philip and his cronies who circled it for months. All those baubles and all that greed. My siblings and I were caught up in the middle of it, hungry and confused kids surrounded by covetous adults spellbound by shiny things.

One of Philip's friends would later tell us that the whole fake burglary had almost been called off mid-crime because the Einstein with the oxy torch filled the house with so much blue smoke while cutting through the door of the safe, that it started billowing out of the windows for the whole suburb to see. Even so, the 'burglars' finished the job with a flourish. Care had been taken to purchase a bag of not inexpensive collectible stamps prior to the burglary. I still have a photo of Philip kneeling on the floor before the disembowelled safe, hundreds of stamps scattered around his feet like confetti, and I imagine some thickie with a criminal record at the end of the operation, emptying the bag on the ground with a flamboyant sweep of his arm and stepping back like an art critic, arms folded, head tilted to the side, to consider the composition. A nice touch that.

Now, the reader may recall that Philip had left us all alone in a motel in Caloundra on that first day after we set out for Hayman Island. Naturally, this was a matter of great interest to the insurance company over the next couple of years as they fought in the courts against making the payout on the grounds that the whole thing stunk to high heaven. Philip always maintained that we had just been hanging out in Caloundra, minding our own business, to break up the drive to Hayman Island, and of course he strongly rejected any suggestion that he had been anywhere near the Gold Coast on the day of the burglary. The problem was that the crack team tasked with staging the burglary were so proud of their work after they had finished, that they retired to the Birdwatchers Bar in Surfers Paradise to sink a few beers in celebration.

I am sure they thought of themselves as something like a sophisticated Michael Caine in *The Italian Job* or (if it had been made then) a Tom Cruise in *Mission Impossible* dangling from a rope between the laser beams. In fact, they were more like a toddler who has found something that smells funny on the front lawn and pokes his finger in it. To wit, while Philip was relaxing in the Birdwatchers Bar watching birds and drinking beer, preparatory to drink-driving back to Caloundra, he got a parking ticket. Incredible. *They only had one job!*

For the next two years Philip lived in an agony of dread that someone would check the records and prove him to be both a liar and a perjurer. And remember, if Normie found out, prison would have been the *least* of Philip's problems.

Anyway, it was clear that the mansion had to go. It had served its purpose and there was no way we could afford it without Normie chipping in, so we moved to a new house in Allawah Street, Sorrento.

A few weeks later I wrote in my diary: *Mum has been very sick. The other day she went to hospital for a day and a night for an abortion. Her second. Philip told her he'd had a vasectomy.*

That was the story. We will never know the truth. I remember Philip taking us to visit Mum at the Gold Coast Hospital where we were told she had undergone a mysterious procedure described to us as a 'curette', and I remember us gathered around her bed wondering what a curette was. With Philip giggling with embarrassment and resting a hand on her shoulder, Mum looked tired and weary and asked us to leave so she could sleep. For many years afterwards we only ever referred to Philip (behind his back, of course) as Vas. Short for vasectomy.

'Where's Vas?'

'In the kitchen making tea'.

'Is Vas home yet?'

'Nah. He's at the races.'

*

The early humans of Eurasia delved deep into tunnels and dark caves to paint images on rock walls, with nothing to light their way except rudimentary torches. When we think of cave art we typically think of the woolly mammoths and shaggy bison of Lascaux but these are no older than about 20,000 years. The earliest cave art in Europe dates back 170,000 years, to a time when the only humans in Europe were our cousins, the Neanderthals. In Bruniquel Cave, in Middle Pleistocene France, a group of them ventured 300 metres into the belly of a mountain. In a broad dark cavern, its walls scratched by the claws of enormous cave bears, they tore 400 stalagmites from the ground and built a series of circular, low-walled structures out of them. In cloying darkness, little family groups stoked comforting fires and, we might assume, huddled together for warmth, told stories and sang songs. What was the point of it all? Were they tripping on drugs or hallucinating after days of isolation in impenetrable darkness? Or was it less complicated? Outside the cave's mouth it was miserably cold, with snow drifts and icy wind. Who can blame them for wanting to disappear into a mountain, to escape all the strife and turmoil, to find a cosy nook where they could be safe, where they could pull a blanket of warm pelts over their heads, take shelter and block out all the bad stuff. In our new house in Sorrento, when I was thirteen, and in many other places as a boy, that is the kind of place that I used to imagine myself crawling into.

11. Fertility Symbols

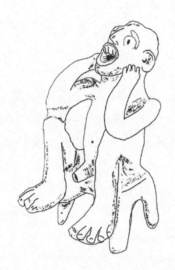

Seated male, Cyprus, c3000 BCE

One of the most striking finds from prehistoric Cyprus (in this case, the Chalcolithic period, being about 3900 to 2400 BCE) is a ceramic model thirty-six centimetres tall of a seated naked male, his feet resting on the front edge of the chair, legs akimbo, affording the observer an unimpeded view of his penis. There are no testicles but at the risk of stating the obvious, it is clearly meant to be a bloke. The model is actually a vessel of some sort, with a hole in the top of the head. You can pour a liquid in the top and it passes through the hollow body and shoots out a hole in the tubular penis. Voila!

The deserved doyen of Cypriot archaeology – Vassos Karageorghis – called the ceramic model 'the ejaculator', which always makes me think of a comic book hero with truly incredible superpowers. The famous zoologist Desmond Morris notes the strained neck muscles (!) and the look of ecstasy (?) and concludes that this is clearly a man in the throes of orgasm. These eminent scholars identify 'the ejaculator' model as a fertility ritual vessel and Morris envisages a farmer strolling his fields of an evening, squirting libations onto the tilled soils through the hollow willy. Whatever is going on, it is a naked man and he is certainly very happy. He has what looks like a big smile on his face (although Karageorghis and Morris see it as more of a grimace). He seems to be joyful.

One pleasant Saturday afternoon when I was fifteen years old and watching television with my thirteen-year-old sister and seventeen-year-old brother, Mum told us all (unsolicited and apropos nothing) that our dad was a premature ejaculator. It is hard to conceive of the silence *that* piece of information was met with by three awkward teenagers. We will never know the truth, but there was rhyme to my mother's reason. Over time, it became my mother's life mission to make my father look bad so that her decisions to stay with Philip seemed a little less incomprehensible. When Mum divorced Dad she insisted it was because of his argumentativeness, dogmatic obstinacy and poor punctuality. Over the years he had morphed into a fully-fledged, salivating sex pervert. Well, if that were true, how do we explain this: in the thick of one of the shitstorms with Philip, when we were poor and desperate, Mum phoned my father out of the blue, and to our enormous surprise, invited him to the Gold Coast from Canberra so that we could all go out to dinner together.

We met up with our father in a Chinese restaurant in Surfers Paradise and the night went by without any arguments. It is probably the only time in my life that I can remember my parents sharing a meal without fighting. Afterwards, while my father waited outside the restaurant expectantly, Mum sat with us in the parked car and floated an idea: how about you kids go back to Canberra for a bit, stay with your dad, just for a little while until I get back on my feet? We shrugged. What the hell else could we do?

Mum beckoned my father over and we wound down the windows. As he leaned forward hopefully there was a kind of thumbs-up from Mum. Dad nodded like a deal had been done, said goodnight to us and walked off into the night. It was understood that we would be seeing him again soon in Canberra. In fact, we didn't see him again for years. Mum changed her mind, I guess.

They made a strange couple. After we moved from Canberra, I remember Dad visiting us in our Isle of Capri house once, our water bed in the next room, canal at the bottom of the garden, where an argument erupted between him, Mum and Philip. John, Sophie and I had all been banished to our bedrooms, permitted one hello when Dad arrived and a goodbye when he left. He hugged me, with Mum watching on critically.

I had listened to their muffled argument through the walls, unsure of what they were saying, and wondering if we might be going back to Canberra after all. That was not to be. Many years later, as an adult, I sat with Dad and talked it over. He told me that he had sent us many birthday and Christmas presents over the years, but they were all returned marked 'not at this address'. We both suspected my mother. What he didn't tell me was what his second wife later shared with me, that he'd had something of a breakdown after his visit to the Isle of Capri. She said that when she met him a year or two later, he was living in a house without electricity. Not because he couldn't afford to pay the bill, but because he lacked the will to. He'd dropped his bundle in a dark and lonely house 1100 kilometres from his children. My stepmother also told us that after she married him and moved into our old house – six years after we had packed our pillowcases and left – all of our kids' clothes were still hanging in our old wardrobes, gathering dust.

Mum may have made the right decision to not send us back with him. She may have made the wrong one. As children all we saw was a father who didn't fight to be in our lives and a mother who was prepared to shunt us onto a man she hated.

*

Before we moved into the house in Sorrento, my grandmother departed once again for her home in Captains Flat, preferring friable asbestos house-cladding to us. She made a very sensible choice. That is not to say that our new home was awful. Quite the opposite. The house had a pool, and a games room downstairs where we could play table tennis and billiards. From the outside we seemed comfortable but a few weeks in, I wrote in my diary: *We have no petrol and no food.*

We stayed in the Sorrento house for about three months and looked ahead to another Christmas with dread. To this day I do not know how the house was being paid for.

Some of the money must have come from Normie and some more came from a hot bible racket. It takes the consummate conman, and one utterly devoid of ethical sentiment (or one with an exquisite sense of irony), to run a scam for dodgy bibles. In September of that year, the month that we moved from the mansion, Philip talked his way into a job as regional manager for a publisher that specialised in Christian literature. Their pièce de resistance was the bible in twelve volumes. The problem was that Philip didn't get off his arse to sell anything. Rather, our garage was stacked from floor to ceiling with boxes of encyclopaedic bibles produced by a company called Zondervan, quality publications with glossy pages and lavishly illustrated. Each box of bibles had someone's name on it: mine, my brother's, my sister's, one for each of my stepsisters, one for my dead uncle, one for my grandmother, others for entirely made-up people. The con was that Philip would 'sell' the bibles to these fictitious purchasers at the recommended retail price and collect his commission, then on-sell them to real people (trusting Christians) at a massive mark-up. It was quite the con, although it is not like Philip had a particular way with words. It wasn't the case that he was some silver-tongued devil, but rather that he never baulked at asking for money. He saw no shame in telling lies for cash.

Words. Words that are spoken and words that are written down. This is the distinction between the 'prehistoric' and the 'historic', a useful distinction, but it masks a chauvinism born of contemporary experience, not of tens of thousands of years of lived reality. There is no qualitative difference between the written and spoken word. We do well to recall that for most of human history it was only when they were voiced – spoken, chanted or sung – that the rhythm, assonance and rhymes of words could be experienced, where the power of words once resided.

We should think of prehistory as ripe with song, a fertile ground for poetry and tall tales, recited and told around campfires and hearths deep into Palaeolithic, Neolithic, Bronze Age and Iron Age nights. Long before there was writing, there were witticisms and puns, priestly invocations that raised goosebumps, soft-whispered love poems that arched backs, laments that brought tears to eyes.

The ancient Greeks knew the power of words and attributed the first poetry to Orpheus, son of Calliope, grandson to Zeus, the son of one of any number of mortal men – the mythical prosopography is murky. Orpheus, the Greeks believed, was married to the chaste Eurydike who died while fleeing a horny demigod, bitten on the heel by a serpent as she ran. As the Greeks told it, the despairing Orpheus followed Eurydike into the shadows of the underworld, descending the many levels of hell, to confront Hades himself and beg for his wife's return. He charmed the evil spirits, drew them to him with his songs, and won the privilege from Hades to lead his wife back into the real world, a living creature, on condition that he never look back to be sure that she was following. He did of course, only to see his wife become insubstantial again and return to the deep. Spurning women from that moment on, heartbroken and scarred, Orpheus invented homosexual love and sang souls into wild beasts. His hymns were so beautiful that the very trees bent over to shade him. He probably deserved better than being torn limb from limb by frenzied women, fresh from a Dionysian orgy, piqued at being excluded from his concert. That's words for you. They can be charming. But words could also get you dismembered.

Philip knew all about the power of words, too. He used them to flatter, manipulate, trick, deceive and con. What made him different from most people was what he called 'the close'. The close was just having the unabashed gall to lure a person into a hole and ask for money, to watch them squirm while you shamed them into committing their hard-earned lolly. He would hold their eye as a kind of challenge. 'You believe me, don't you? Or are you calling me a liar?' All the while, lying.

To do that, you need to feel nothing. To do that, you need to be able to do as Philip did – laugh at people who are easily beguiled by words and scorn them for their feeble-minded trust. It never occurred to Philip that it was *his* fault that they were losing their savings. To Philip it was their fault – for believing.

For several weeks in Sorrento, we watched Philip launch another round of barbecues and marathon drinking sessions staged beside our enticing pool, while we played billiards and table tennis in the evening. But Philip was slipping. He naively thought that if he just held it together for a while, the insurance payout on the burglary would come through.

Of course, the insurance company withheld payment and instead, a criminal investigation was in the offing. As the weeks progressed, we saw less of him. There were more and more nights when Philip would just leave us, go into town and come home late, slurring and smelling of alcohol. The drunkenness became drunken surliness, and inevitably there were more arguments. They were violent, venomous arguments that I would hear late at night as a sinister murmur through my bedroom wall. And there were the peculiar, deranged threats: 'I can kill you if I want to.' 'I'll throw you off the balcony.' 'Nobody could stop me if I want to kill you.' 'I'll kill your children and make you watch.' 'We'll all die in a ring of flames.'

Philip made it to Christmas and to prove that there really are Christmas miracles, he made it through to the other side. I even got a couple of presents. But on the night of 30 December Philip went out for 'a drink', another drink in a downward spiral of 'going out'. We were all on edge, knowing the signs well by now, anticipating, feeling the tension in the belly. I went to bed that night, and as he hadn't yet come home, I fell asleep easily enough. It was just one of those nights. We would have to ride it out. But I remember Mum waking me later in the pitch dark, gently shaking my shoulder, whispering into my ear to keep quiet. Without turning on the lights, she led me through the hallway to my sister's room, the only room in the house with a lock on the door, where my brother and sister were waiting. Perfunctorily, Mum explained: Philip was home and raging. We were going to sleep the night there with the door locked.

I had my pillow with me, and I lay on the carpeted floor and fell asleep. My brother did the same, while Mum curled up on my sister's bed with Sophie, waiting for the new day. It was a poor sleep, fitful and disturbed, the hard floor numbing my shoulder, so I was only half-asleep when I heard the firm knock at the door, the sound of the locked doorhandle half-turning in the darkness, and my stepfather's angry voice: 'Open the door.' We all lay there silently. Nobody moved. Nobody breathed. Then a strange thing happened. My drunken stepfather found our poor happy dopey golden retriever, stood him outside the door and gee'd him into a lather of confused growls and barks. Then, out of ideas, silence. We heard Philip stumble downstairs where he collapsed on his bed in an alcoholic coma. At dawn, we let ourselves out and began slinking about the house like ninjas. I expected that we would hit the road again, but Mum didn't tell us to start packing. I think she felt that if we could just make it through to the evening, after Philip had had a chance to sleep it off ...

That morning, as we tippy-toed in and out of our bedrooms as quietly as possible, the telephone rang. I can still hear the metallic ring, see all of us freeze, turn to the phone.

'Quick!' Mum hissed as I ran over to it, snatching it up after maybe three rings.

It was the Zondervan director of sales. He asked for Philip. Sotto voce, I told him that Philip wasn't in, but then Philip's voice broke in on the other line. He had picked up the extension in his bedroom downstairs. I hung up and turned to Mum.

'He's awake,' I said with dread.

Downstairs we could hear Philip screaming at the poor

Zondervan fellow. I don't recall the precise words, but to paraphrase, it went something like: 'Get fucked!'

I can only begin to imagine the bewilderment on the other end of the line from a man who had hitherto only known Philip as a God-loving Christian who would belt out 'This is the Day that the Lord Has Made' at bible meetings.

Meanwhile, we waited in trepidation. Finally, the shouting stopped and Philip came upstairs with a heavy tread, bleary-eyed and yellow from the drink. When he saw Mum, she hastened to mollify him. She offered to make him breakfast, his favourite fry-up, and with gentle words she manoeuvred him back downstairs so that he could 'have a nap'. He said very little, angrily allowing himself to be persuaded to go back to bed, but watchful from under his heavy lids. When Mum came back a few minutes later, we set to madly gathering up our belongings, cramming them into our school bags. We were preparing to make the dash when Philip came back upstairs and saw what we were doing. It was one of those hold-your-breath moments where it could have gone either way. We all just stood there quietly waiting for time to right itself, to resume its old familiar one beat per second. In the end, amazingly, morosely, he told us to leave: 'Get the hell out of my house.'

He didn't have to tell us twice. Coolly, methodically, professionally we dispersed rapidly to our respective bedrooms and continued to snatch up the essentials. Undies, t-shirts, socks. We gathered again in the loungeroom around Mum, holding our bags, Philip watching in menacing silence. When Mum picked up the car keys Philip said nothing, but as we headed for the stairwell that led to the front door, he changed his mind and snarled, 'You're not having the car.' He snatched the keys from Mum's hand and shook her, but in a moment of self-awareness he paused. Imagine a sunken loungeroom connected to the dining room by three little steps, the kitchen behind a wooden slatted partition, a balcony on one side (one that Philip had recently threatened to throw Mum off), a television in the corner, the stairwell, a creamy shag pile carpet, a mother and her three children clutching their worldly possessions to their chests, and a grown man standing in the centre of it all, the spiel point of all the chaos and suffering, wearing nothing but a pair of canary-yellow Y-fronted bikini briefs. He turned and walked to the stairwell to get his clothes on in the bedroom, still holding the keys, and bizarrely we quietly followed him, because the bedroom was down a short hallway from the front door. We reached the bottom of the stairs and the instant he disappeared into his bedroom, Mum opened the door and we all streamed through it.

Running for it. Again. Like all the other times, feeling the same feelings again, but each time feeling them incrementally worse. More humiliation. More degradation. Greater fear. A swelling anger. Grinding sadness. Insupportable resentment. Uncertainty. Not quite fourteen years old and powerless. Like anybody who has swum in the rolling Pacific Ocean I had been dumped, experienced that sensation of being taken by a giant wave and hurled back to the shore, completely out of control, thumped against the hard sandy bottom, held there. I had learned how to relax, how to submit my body to the turbulent waters, be pulled and buffeted. I had learned how to hold my breath and wait for it to pass. That morning, I held my breath. As we ran, Philip came charging back out of the bedroom, still in his Y-fronts, and Mum slammed the front door behind us.

We were well into the front garden before Philip burst through the door, lunged at Mum and grabbed her by the wrists. She wrestled and screamed, 'Let me go, leave me alone,' as we three children watched on, mortified. Philip held both Mum's wrists in his left hand and raised his right hand to strike her. Cars on the street slowed down. A man walking his dog paused to see what the commotion was all about. People were watching from windows across the road. He didn't throw the punch.

Perhaps Philip felt vulnerable, or finally, he felt ridiculous, so he backed up in his yellow undies, with his bloated beer belly, skinny legs, appendix scar, his terrified wife and stepchildren and an audience of the neighbourhood. He tried to drag Mum into the house but she pulled and struggled to escape his grasp, so he turned and hurried back inside to get his gear on for real this time. The front door closed after him and we scarpered across the garden, jumped the garden beds separating our home from the neighbours, and ran to their front door. Even as it was happening, as we ran for our lives, hearts pounding, I was conscious of the ludicrousness of it all and vaguely aware that time was ticking away and that if it went on for too much longer, I would be bigger, my brother would be bigger, and we would not be the victims anymore.

Mum knocked on the neighbour's door. We waited. And then an angel opened it. A middle-aged woman, cool and calm. Mum collapsed through her front door begging for help: 'My husband's trying to kill me.' The woman just stepped back and ushered us in, casually shutting the door and locking it. We sat down in her dining room full of frilly tablecloths and flowery placemats, where she made Mum a cup of tea and spoke with her softly and reassuringly. She looked like someone with experience, maybe a social worker or a past survivor of domestic violence herself. Whatever the reason, she seemed totally unconcerned about Philip. 'You'll be fine in here,' she said, and I didn't doubt it for a moment. She gave me lemon cordial, the fluorescent 1980s kind. It was like we had entered another dimension. I never learned that woman's name and never saw her again, but she saved our bacon that day. There are many people who would have shut the door in our faces, left us to our fates, and many others had done exactly that over the years. Instead, she opened her door to us. It seemed so simple to her. And so, we stayed for a long time, Mum sipping her tea with trembling hands at the kitchen table, our neighbour listening quietly as Mum nervously shared her fears and sorrows, and in that whole time, maybe an hour, we saw nothing of Philip. He hadn't worked out where we were, but it was only a matter of time before he did, so Mum once again called Joan and asked her to pick us up. Astute readers will note that Mum did not call the police. Why not? Well, that burglary, you see. And Normie, who didn't much like people who had dealings with the police. When Joan pulled up, we hustled out to her car, watched by our guardian angel in a brick-veneer house in Sorrento.

We spent the night at Joan's house and the next morning (New Year's Day) we moved back into the Salvation Army refuge. My third time. Happy new year. In the kerfuffle we had left our bags behind. We were literally left with nothing but the clothes we were standing in.

*

If the geneticists are not getting it completely wrong, most Europeans have rather a lot of Neanderthal DNA in them. When I first studied the Neanderthals, we were confidently instructed that they predated modern humans by thousands of years, then mysteriously died out, which was lucky for Homo sapiens because it meant we could swoop into an empty Europe and fill the void. We now know that modern humans and Neanderthals co-existed for millennia, and that Neanderthals were fun at parties. At least, that is what I am surmising from the fact that a lot of copulation seems to have taken place between the two species. What is more, a study of our mitochondrial DNA strongly suggests that the sex was not just between robust Neanderthal males and gracile sapiens females. Rather, a fair deal of sex involved female Neanderthals and male Homo sapiens. If we consider the evidence that the structure of the Neanderthal throat might have prevented them from even being able to speak, coupled with the heavy brows and protuberant noses, the DNA in our bodies today is genetic evidence that some sapiens are not particularly fussy.

Philip was one of them. At forty-four years old, having turfed us out on the street, he took in a twenty-six-year-old sex worker. Our sources told us she lived in our house for several weeks, while we were doing our time with the Salvos, and she nursed Philip through a medical crisis: he came home paralytic drunk one night and put his foot through a glass sliding door, and the wound got infected. Trouble in paradise.

But relationships for violent alcoholics have a pretty low success rate and we were told that after a couple of months Philip and his lover had a massive row and he tried to throw her out. When she didn't budge, Philip went into town and brought home two *more* prostitutes, telling her she was no longer welcome because he was sleeping with them that night. She never stood a chance. It was basic arithmetic.

All through this we were catching our breath in the Salvation Army refuge. We never really felt safe there because Philip knew where it was from our previous sojourn, but he never came by. We were all wearing Salvation Army hand-me-downs at this time so when we received some good intel that Philip was out of the house for a few hours we ventured back to pick up our stuff. It was like the *Mary Celeste* if the *Mary Celeste* had been a bordello. I went into my bedroom. The sheets were twisted up on the mattress. There was an empty wine glass beside the bed with lipstick on the rim. I felt degraded and hollow. A perfect stranger had been resting her head on my pillow! I recall seeing a small canister-thing on the windowsill above the bed. Picking it up between my thumb and forefinger I read the label: spermicide.

Sex, today and in prehistory, at least for many people, is cause for joy – healthy, profound, amusing, binding, ridiculous, fun, comforting, embarrassing, confusing, enriching, but in the wrong hands, a destructive weapon. With Philip around it always felt dirty and sordid. As a kid there was Philip and prostitutes, his friends and prostitutes, alcohol and prostitutes.

Sometime later, when we had left the Salvation Army refuge, Mum confronted Philip with what she had heard about the sex worker. Philip puffed himself up with indignation and declared: 'I never slept with that woman!' When pressed he said dismissively, 'Besides, I threw her out.' Mum replied, 'You do that with all your women'.

12. A Nice Broad Beach

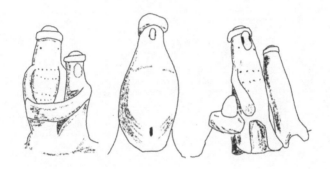

Family scenes, Pierides Bowl,
Cyprus, 2000–1750 BCE

We spent three weeks at the Salvation Army refuge that third time. After the initial sense of failure and despondency, we settled into a routine. Philip was off the scene and, refreshingly, incredibly, Mum showed no inclination to find him or to be found by him. The refuge was in an old part of Southport, away from the tacky chrome and superficial spangle of Surfers Paradise. I liked it. It felt like a home. There was a sense that people in the street had settled there, raised children in it. But, of course, they all knew about the house that we were living in and what sort of people used it. I recall walking out the front gate with my brother one day as an old lady passed by, trailing a shopping buggy on wheels. She smiled politely, even kindly, and said good morning, but on her face and in her eyes was the unmistakable look of pity.

It was the school holidays. Other kids were going to the beach, catching movies, holidaying interstate, riding bicycles in the street out the front, inviting friends around for sleepovers. I sat on the back step of a Salvation Army refuge and read books or watched the television quietly, wondering vaguely how long a charity lets desperate people live in their housing facilities before they politely ask them to leave. I went to a corner-store barber one morning and as he snipped away at my 1980s mop, he made polite conversation. He asked me where I lived and I didn't know what to say. Finally, I told him I had just moved into the big white house on the corner. He nodded kindly, said nothing, kept combing and snipping. At the end, I held out my money and he politely refused it. He knew what the big white house on the corner was.

Surprisingly, in the three weeks that we were in the refuge we had it almost completely to ourselves. As the days turned into weeks Mum started thinking about how we might get back on our feet. Again, she floated the idea of us kids moving back to Canberra, strategising vaguely about how we might return on our own to live with our father for a bit, while she stayed on the Gold Coast to work things out. Then we ran into a slightly creepy bible-seller from Zondervan and he offered, in the spirit of Christian charity, to take us kids into his home in Brisbane to give Mum some breathing space. Even Mum thought better of it when he said he was only interested in taking in my brother and me, not Sophie.

In the end, Mum did call my father in Canberra and asked him for the bond on a new rental unit. He paid it and we moved into a two-bedroom dive on Surf Parade in Broadbeach. The wallpaper was stained and peeling. I remember all of the furniture in that unit: four dining chairs with timber frames, the lacquer flaking off, and fading brown covers; a round lacquered dining table; a velveteen brown sofa with fat armrests, wearing at the front so that you could see the yellow foam peeking out from under the upholstery; a narrow upright credenza; a double bed in one room with a surprisingly ornate brass bedhead; a small double bed in the other room with solid springs under the thin lumpy mattress; and a washing machine. Modest but sufficient, though after dark the scuttle of enormous cockroaches in the kitchen was plainly audible.

Mum and Sophie shared the double bed in one room. John and I took turns enjoying the luxury of the second bedroom. On the off week, I would sleep on the lounge. We had a few changes of clothes, some sheets, a saucepan and frying pan, and a few plates.

It is a measure of how low we had sunk that I wrote in my diary that the new place was 'really nice'. A week later I turned fourteen.

*

Chapman, Mawson, Torrens, Isle of Capri, Paradise Point, Surfers Paradise, Rialto, Broadbeach Waters, Mermaid Waters, Sorrento, Southport, Broadbeach. It had been quite the ride. But there were ghosts in Broadbeach. Not the kind that play electric organs on New Year's Eve but a different kind, all but obliterated now by the high-rises of the Gold Coast tourist scene. Back in 1963 some soil contractors who were stripping deposits in Broadbeach (actually, closer to Mermaid Beach now), turned up human bones. In the end, archaeologists exposed some 150 humans of both sexes and all ages. Most peculiarly, the bodies had been disarticulated – defleshed, the skeleton taken apart and buried in little stacks in shallow pits. The long bones were arranged vertically around the sides of each small, roughly circular niche, with the smaller bones (ribs, fingers, toes, lower jaw) placed inside, and all of it surmounted by the toothy cranium. The burial ground was used by Aboriginal people until after the white invasion, and maybe for 1000 years before that. It is evidence of incredible continuity of tradition, if the carbon dates can be believed (radiocarbon dating was in its infancy). So, what was so special about that place? Did it catch the breeze? Could you see the migrating whales from there? Or was it just soft earth to dig into? And how do you bring yourself to watch the flesh rot off the skeleton of your dead granny, hubby or toddler, pull the bones apart and make a sculpture out of them?

Broadbeach today is a place of fun and laughter. Joy. Beautiful beaches, bars and nightclubs, fine restaurants, five-star hotels. But it has always been a sad place for me. Even now I feel a dark cloud descend when I drive past the address of my old block of flats, even though it has long since been demolished and replaced with a multi-storey building. Parts of my past in Broadbeach have been erased. I share that much with the descendants of the Australian Aboriginals buried at the Broadbeach burial ground.

*

One week after we moved into the Broadbeach unit, one week after we left the Salvation Army refuge for the third time, I started a new school year. For me it was the beginning of Grade 9, for Sophie the start of Grade 7 and her final year in primary school, and for John the start of Grade 11. It was a surreal experience, dressing in my uniform in the morning and making the thirty-minute walk to Merrimac State High School, sitting in class with the other kids who seemed to have no concerns. These conventional and unremarkable things were, to us, daily little miracles achieved in the face of extraordinary events. I would hang out with my friends at lunch, talking and joking or playing murderous games of Red Rover, but none of my pals had the slightest clue of what was going on in my life after school hours. They seemed so relaxed about school pick-ups, while I remained hyper-aware of the clock ticking down to the 3 pm bell, when I would have to leave my safe haven and walk home, wondering if Philip had tracked us down yet.

And then, six weeks later, he did track us down. John and I would walk home from school together before meeting up with Sophie about halfway. I imagined that Mum spent each day alone, hunched in our little unit, chain smoking, sipping cups of tea and obsessing about all the errors of judgement that had led us to Broadbeach. In fact, although she did that most days, on other days she struck up a bizarre, short-lived and ill-defined 'dating' relationship with a BMW-driving spiv named Stefan who occupied the fringes of Philip's world.

On the way home from school early in the school year, and as we approached the bus stop beside a small shopping centre that has since become the sprawling Pacific Fair, we saw Philip waiting with Sophie. He looked hungover, angry and vindictive. Sophie hurried anxiously over to us and Philip rose to his feet and followed her. We were always going to be his way of finding Mum. We were the weak link. He just had to be patient, wait outside our school, and follow us home one day. I do not recall being surprised to see him there, just disappointed. As John and I slowed our pace, Philip strode over and started issuing threats. 'Tell your mother to call me in one hour,' he demanded coolly, 'or there will be trouble.' He wagged his finger and walked away, glancing menacingly back over his shoulder.

Mum's solution was to get John to call Philip instead, which resulted in my sixteen-year-old brother being screamed at over the phone before Philip hung up in his ear. So, with a feeling of sinking inevitability, I sat in our little loungeroom (my bedroom) and watched as Mum picked up the phone and with her long-nailed fingers dialled his number, which had been *our* number just a couple of months before. Of course, Philip had heard about Stefan and the man who I'd never met, who drove a BMW with (Mum had boasted) a sunroof, became the focus of the bizarre argument that followed. I listened in horror and despair and jotted in my diary some of the barbs that Mum and Philip exchanged. When Philip screamed, 'I forbid you to see another man,' Mum replied with cool self-possession, 'You lost your rights to me a long time ago'. Philip countered this news with the time-honoured response: 'I'll have both his legs broken.' It all ended with phones being slammed down.

Mum sat back on the lounge, struck a match and lit a cigarette looking very smug, confiding in us that it had been her plan all along to use Stefan as a way of getting back at Philip. She rose and strutted about the unit like she had won something. She had won nothing. She was losing … her exhausted children. We were growing older and sadly, less forgiving, less accepting, and although we wanted to love Mum we were becoming ever more resentful as our respect for her seeped away.

The next day we went to school as usual, sat through English classes, art classes, science classes, but I heard very little of it over the relentless tick-tick-tick of the clock on the wall counting down to when I would be home again. Almost all of my memories from this time involve summer heat, high blue skies and puffy white clouds, and the tang of sea salt in the air that we breathed off the ocean just a couple of hundred metres from the Broadbeach unit. When the bell rang in the afternoon, John and I met at the school gate and started the walk home, picking Sophie up on the way. At this time, we were still not entirely sure that Philip knew where we lived, so we were watchful. Not long after meeting Sophie we spied him cruising by us in his car. We abruptly changed direction to put him off the scent and walked quickly down another street, zigzagging towards home. We paused a block from our unit and watched and waited. We were three kids trying to evade a violent grown man, to protect our mum. To protect ourselves. There was nothing funny about it, no giggling or eye-rolling. It was not a game.

After a while, we were sure that we had given him the slip, but as we briskly walked the final 100 metres and turned into our driveway, we heard a cocky toot-toot from a car horn. We turned to see Philip parked in a side street where he had been waiting for us under a pine tree. He started his car and drove off with a stupid grin on his face, giving us a cheeky little 'gotcha' wave as he went. I recall it as a terribly deflating moment. And now we knew that he knew where we lived.

Two nights later, Mum called an old friend and suggested that they have a night out together, to let off steam. She made it all sound so innocent and spontaneous. She left her three children at home to fret and ruminate as she tottered out that Friday night in her high heels. We knew what was coming. Of course she manufactured a reason to visit all of Philip's old haunts, and in spite of the prostitutes, the spermicide, the Salvation Army refuge, the threats, when she found him in some seedy Gold Coast nightclub she struck up a conversation. The next morning, Philip knocked at our door. He looked simultaneously smug and sheepish as Mum opened it, feigning surprise, and ushered him into our loungeroom and back into our lives.

I have seen a nature documentary about a species of eagle that plays out dangerous courtship games in the mating season. The male and the female catch the updrafts to incredible heights, link talons and dice with death by spiralling back to earth locked in a fatal embrace. But the thing about the eagles is that they let go of each other at the last second, spread glorious wings, and fly. After all, anything else is suicidal madness. But there was Philip, walking across our modest threshold again, sitting in our loungeroom, sipping tea from one of our few teacups, hooded eyes glancing around the room, passing silent judgement on our peeling wallpaper, the threadbare armrests, the worn carpet, and locking talons with Mum in a crazy downward spiral.

He left us alone twice during the day, returning each time with sheets, crockery and books from the Sorrento home, re-entering our loungeroom each time, giggling and beaming as if he was doing us a favour by returning our own belongings to us. Between carloads, Mum would try to reassure us that she had no interest in him at all and that there was no way that there would be a reconciliation. We listened silently, made no comment, knowing that there was nothing that we could say to stop them doing whatever they wanted to do anyway. The only good thing that I can say about that day is that we had more teacups by the end of it than when it started.

The next day Philip was back, still with the goofy smile and the giggles that were so at odds with how we were feeling. No doubt he had worked out what was, in my view, the main strength of our new home: it was too small for him to move in. When he insisted on taking us out to lunch, John told him he wasn't interested. The rest of us trooped into Surfers Paradise where we were shouted lunch and then a ride on a waterslide in a pale imitation of a fun family day out. I recall thinking that it was too cold for the waterslide and then the sour, guilty feeling when I accepted Philip's offer to buy me the ticket for a ride. But I also remember being too scared to say no, stripping off my t-shirt, collecting my surf mat and trudging mirthlessly up the stairs to the top. It was a strange feeling, spinning around in a wet tube just weeks after leaving the refuge and on the cusp of Philip's easy and graceless return to the fold.

The thing about waterslides is that although you may feel alone as you slip down long runs and into blind curves, with nothing but a ceiling of blue sky above you, or slosh through dark tunnels accompanied by nothing but the distant squeals of children and the gurgle of water, there is always, inevitably, the point where you pop out the other end, into stark bright day, and your stepfather is standing there waiting, with his cold, bloodshot eyes.

Philip was on his best behaviour those first two days, but the next day he came back to our unit looking for trouble. There were arguments and threats and when Philip snarled at Mum and growled at John, John held his eye. A dangerous miscalculation. Philip walked over to him and struck him hard across the face. John took it in silence, turned on his heel and went into the bedroom. Surely *this* would be the straw that broke the camel's back? *This* would be the point at which my mother said to herself, 'No more'?

But no. Philip was back the next day, obsequious and toadying, filling our little unit with his insidious lies and poorly concealed rage. The next day, he insisted on going with Mum to the house of one of her few remaining friends and, as perpetrators of domestic violence the world over do, he picked a fight with the friend and destroyed the friendship with cool calculation, thereby isolating Mum further from anybody who could help her.

We yo-yo'd from anger and threats to giggles and glad-handing. There was nothing we children could do about it. We just watched his comings and goings helplessly, and with nowhere to hide in that tiny unit, I withdrew into myself instead, blanked him out as he walked through our door uninvited and shamelessly ate our food. Two days later he was all smiles and confected kindness again when he apologetically explained that he would not be able to bring over any of our belongings from the Sorrento home that day because he was busy looking for work. A couple of hours after he left us, Mum dressed herself up and went into town to check all the bars. She found Philip half-drunk in one of them and threw a glass of brandy over his head before storming out. It was more of that death spiral, the locked talons, and the incomprehensible inability to just release and fly away.

By 2 am, Philip was back, drunk and seething. I lay on the lounge (my bed) with my eyes closed for two hours as Mum and Philip attacked each other in suppressed screams under the single fluorescent tube above the kitchen table, just a couple of metres from my bed/the lounge. I spent the whole two hours waiting for the punches that never came and listening to his death threats, each one delivered in a low, level voice. He would murder Mum. He would break her nose and make her ugly. He would burn down her house. He would kill her children while she watched.

At 4 am he left and I lapsed into a sleep of relief, pleased that he was gone, but when I awoke three hours later Philip was asleep on one of our dining chairs, chin on his chest, his feet resting on another chair pulled up opposite him. Presumably, he had tapped at the door during the night or whispered through Mum's window. All that I knew for sure was that Mum had let him back in, the man who had spent two hours threatening to murder her children.

Philip's dark and angry presence always felt like an invasion. It was no more than five paces from the front door through our loungeroom and into our tiny kitchen, but it was ours. To enter it, you had to cross a threshold, pass our blue-green door, faded by the Gold Coast sun. The threshold is known to anthropologists as a liminal space, neither inside nor out, neither initiated nor uninitiated, neither private nor civic, but critical to all of these things. In many cultures, the threshold is revered because it separates the sacred interior from the profane.

In our home, there was a little less reverence. In the evenings, Philip would cross our threshold without invitation, without knocking. We would not greet him, there were no words of welcome. He would move across that tiny loungeroom, unlit cigarette in his mouth, and make his way to the stove. Forever losing his lighter, Philip would turn on a hotplate and leaning forward he would touch the tip of the cigarette to the burning surface. He would draw on it until the tip glowed, stand, inhale, exhale in a long smoky breath, before sitting down at our table. A perversion of domesticity.

Late one evening when he did that, in a bad mood, Philip turned on John. Snarling, he came at John with a clenched right fist, ready for a fight. But as Philip lunged at him, John snatched up a long, curved boomerang – a childhood gift decorated with kitsch, painted kangaroos – and stared him down, locked and loaded. A storm was building. Philip backed down but there had been a shift. His voice was quavering as he issued his parting threat. We were still scared, but this time, he was scared too.

13. The Sunshine State

'The Harvester Vase', Crete, 1550–1450 BCE

After his night on the dining room chairs, Philip left us alone for a couple of days, but the spiral soon recommenced. Ever the big talker, he boasted that we needn't worry, because he was buying a new house. This fantasy stuff was falling on deaf ears by now. Unbelievably, despite the increasing upheavals, Philip's daughters (my stepsisters) came to visit us from Sydney! As they walked into our place and pursed their lips in judgement, I felt humiliated. I wanted to shout, 'Your father did this to us!' But we said nothing, and John and I surrendered our bed for the two teenaged girls, pulling together two armchairs to make a bed of sorts for ourselves to sleep in. It came as no surprise to us when Philip left them with us later in the day and went off on a bender. It was about 3 am when he came home, staggering drunk and intent on violence. He thumped on the door, but we were too scared to open it. I could see him outside the big front window, pacing backwards and forwards in the dim light like a wild animal, a beast caged for too long. There was a pause.

'Open the door', he demanded coolly. We didn't, so he bent down and picked up a pot plant and with all his strength he hurled it through the window. The glass exploded, his daughters screamed, my mother wailed, and as the glass tinkled I watched the pot roll across the loungeroom floor, spilling its contents of black dirt in a dark arc. Then another explosion of glass and screaming. He had picked up a second pot plant and hurled it through one of the bedroom windows. There was another pause, more ranting, then another pot plant through another window.

We lived in a block of four flats arranged in a line with us on the end, a vacant lot on either side, but there were maybe twenty other units within fifty metres of our house. Nobody came to help us, which was wise. Nobody called the police, which is baffling. My stepsisters, knowing that they would be on a plane home in a couple of days, didn't care who heard. They screamed and swore at Philip while my brother and I – more experienced in these matters – tried to shut them down, until finally an off-duty policeman ran over, long pants, bare feet and no shirt, and I heard my stepfather's heavy tread as he scarpered.

I can still remember the look on his face. At first, the cold anger, but as he smashed each window, methodically, one by one, with us cringing in fear, he changed. As the screaming reached its highest pitch, he was giggling. Why? Because he loved it. I said that he paced like a caged animal, but of course it was we who were caged, and he held the key. It was his violence. And he was laughing as he destroyed our home because he loved the sense of power it gave him.

This is how I remember the next morning: about an hour after sunrise, after a sleepless night, while waiting for the window repair shops to open, we surveyed the damage. Black dirt was sprayed across the loungeroom floor mixed with fragments of thick window glass. The window frames were empty and bird noises and car engines could be heard. A gentle breeze blew. I sat there in dread of when the neighbours would wake up and we would be the objects of their anger and pity and scorn. And then Philip called our telephone and demanded (*demanded!*) to see his daughters, like the situation had been one of *our* making. When he arrived, they walked out the door to meet their father who was waiting in the driveway. I never saw my stepsisters again.

We took the day off school. We had nothing worth stealing so we just drew the curtains over the empty window frames and, slinking out of the front door, we caught an early bus into Surfers Paradise where we sipped milkshakes for breakfast and waited as Mum called around to find a window repair man. Remarkably, we had the windows installed just a few hours later, probably paid for by my father, and we headed back home to await the next onslaught. We heard nothing from the landlord. We were back at school the next day.

Four days later Mum and Philip were on the phone to each other, whirling once more in their wild, obsessive death spiral, we three children swirling around with them, clinging on to their parents' ankles for dear life, eyes screwed shut, silently gritting their teeth, hoping, waiting for it all to stop.

*

One of the biggest ironies in our lives at this time was that the heartbreak and strife were taking place in a wonderland full of happy and carefree holidaymakers. A transient population of tourists washed into and out of the Gold Coast, ebbing and flowing with the seasons and school holidays through the population of locals. The mundane permanence of the residents existed in parallel with the footloose world of the out-of-towners. I was always painfully aware that while we were sweeping shards of broken glass off our worn carpet, other people were taking romantic walks on the beach, flying down rollercoasters or attending aerobics classes. Aerobics was the rage back then. A curly-headed, toothy American named Richard Simmons made a fortune out of losing weight and then berating others to do the same thing. He did it all on TV, smiling through the pain, and women flocked to aerobics classes in pastel 1980s leotards in the same way that people go to yoga and Pilates today.

Call me a cynic, but it was probably much the same in the Indus civilisation in the third millennium BCE, only without the lycra, when yogis seem to have exerted some kind of power over people. Ancient seals from around 2500 BCE depict a male figure, sometimes with three faces, seated cross-legged on a low stool with his heels together in the classic yoga pose, bangles down the length of his arms.

Other artwork of the period shows people in various yoga poses, familiar even today, an illustration of the incredible durability of some recreational activities, especially those that bring serenity and happiness (and rooms full of people doing the downward dog). Classic yoga includes meditation and a spiritual coming together of mind and body, a form of uber-relaxation. A little light exercise and peace of mind have clearly brought the human race joy for a very long time. (Sticklers may note that technically, the Indus civilisation was not a prehistoric society and outside the scope of a book called *Prehistoric Joy*, but the writing used by the people of ancient Mohenjo-Daro, Harappa and other towns in the Indus valley in the 1200 years from 3000 BCE has never been translated. Some would disagree with me, but when one linguist can look at a short piece of text and translate it as 'Here is the tribute offered to the god Kueya' and another can look at the same piece of text and translate it as 'The aquatic birds have covered all the waterways', you know you have got a problem.)

As those tourists would amble back to their hotels from the beach, they would cross the vacant lot outside our front door, sandy towels slung over one shoulder, licking ice creams and laughing in family groups or romantic couples. We were often visible through our front door. Sometimes they gawped at us but mostly they were oblivious. Their heads were full of fun and music. They were full of joy, and it was impossible sometimes not to be jealous and resentful of them, in the same way that it was hard not to be envious of my school friends, some of whom were already going to the local nightclubs with a pocketful of money given to them by generous parents, to experiment with girls and underaged drinking. The groups of cheerful tourists strolling home across that vacant lot, shifting from summer beach to luxurious hotel, remind me now of the men depicted on the Harvester Vase – a Minoan Greek vessel dating to about 1550 BCE. Some twenty-seven men are shown in relief, walking home from the fields after a day in the sun, sheaths of wheat and threshing forks over shoulders, mouths open in song, one man holding a sistrum, an ancient percussion instrument that made a rattly-jingly sound something like a tambourine. We could only look on at the end of the long hot day at the shared joy of the passing tourists, their friendly company and shared laughter a rebuke, as we sat in our grubby unit.

Some evenings we would hear the doof doof doof of distant music from parties and the nightclubs at the Gold Coast Casino, just a couple of hundred metres away. We could imagine the dancing bodies, the bump and grind, the spinning disco balls, the voices raised over the music. All that happiness. The noise was usually distant, and the scene felt utterly unattainable to me.

*

Humans love their music, musicians, and their musical instruments, be they electric guitar or, as it was in the late 1980s, awful synthesiser and moany saxophone. In the Cycladic Islands in the Aegean around 2500 BCE the lyre was the instrument of choice for testosterone-charged young men looking to impress the ladies. Some of the world's loveliest prehistoric art comes from the Cyclades. Human figures in white polished marble, heads tilted back, serene faces upraised. The Cycladic figures were most commonly highly stylised, naked women, but occasionally a male musician was depicted, seated, the same impassive uplifted face, with lyre resting on their lap, a testament to the power of music to bring humans joy. But of the many Cycladic figures in collections around the world, a large proportion are unprovenanced, and sadly, a great many of them are forgeries. The problem is so serious that archaeologists typically exclude Cycladic finds from serious analysis unless they can be demonstrated definitively to have come from sanctioned excavations. In the case of the assemblage from one prehistoric workshop – that of the so-called Goulandris Sculptor – that reduces the number of figurines from seventy-six to a dismal four. In other words, seventy-two of the figurines attributed to the Goulandris Sculptor are either fakes or looted material, or authentic, but impossible to demonstrate to be authentic (which is perhaps just as sad). Forging a work of prehistoric art is an unforgivable piece of deceit, a fraud committed against the shared human experience, a lie about what constitutes, and has always constituted, happiness. Not to my stepfather, Philip. Philip would have found it funny.

Another classic work of art from the Indus valley, a couple of centuries either side of 2000 BCE, illustrates how humans have also derived joy from dancing since prehistory, just like the Gold Coast holidaymakers – unless the so-called 'Dancing Girl' from Mohenjo-Daro has been incorrectly named. The Dancing Girl rests on one leg, looking incredibly sassy, her big eyes lidded seductively, one bangled arm resting on her hip just above her in-yer-face Mappa Tassie. She is naked except for a necklace and those bangles but she has an incredible hairdo, a thick plait pulled up diagonally behind her head. I kept a date with her in the National Museum in Delhi several years ago. Some builders were at work in the next gallery and one of them – dressed in raggedy clothes and dirty from his work – wandered in and stood in front of the Dancing Girl for a good five minutes. Middle-class white tourists with years of expensive education under their belts strolled by her blithely, fresh from their air-conditioned coaches, and paid her little attention, but the labourer was transfixed. I could understand why. The Dancing Girl is compelling and captivating, small at only 10.5 centimetres tall, but embodying an indefinable power, mighty because of her femaleness and nudity, not vulnerable because of it.

*

My mother loved dancing. She was a teenager in the 1950s and a young woman in her twenties in the 1960s. Mum would often reminisce about the country dances she attended in her youth, innocent fun when eligible bachelors would compete for her attention and she would dance until her feet were sore. I have memories of Mum dancing while doing the vacuuming and of her swaying her hips and singing under her breath while making the dinner. When I was a child at weddings and parties, when she had exhausted her other dancing partners, she would make me feel very grown up by dancing with me. She would lead me onto the dance floor holding my soft kiddie hands in her warm adult ones and she would twist and jitterbug, encouraging me not to be shy, throwing her head back and laughing. This was my Mum at her best, without a care in the world, uninhibited and happy, holding me in the waltz, looking down at me adoringly, making me feel loved. She felt alive and lively, strong and fun. This was a time before Philip, when I was a child, when my mother was everything to me.

Mum's relationship with Philip was doomed for many reasons; one of them was that Philip was a terrible dancer. In fact, he was oddly unaffected by music. I have no memory of him being moved by it, or being moved by anything much at all. I suppose Philip must have read the newspaper from time to time, or a book or magazine, but I have no recollection of it. He never read poetry, never went to the theatre, an art gallery or the ballet. There were no weekend trips to the museum. He showed no interest in the nightly news, politics or world events. Drunk or sober, he seemed to lack all empathy. He thought nothing of stealing money from an elderly widow, for the same reason that a Delhi labourer pausing in a museum for five minutes to gaze with curiosity at the Dancing Girl of Mohenjo-Daro would have been incomprehensible to him – because outside of himself, people weren't really all that important to him. And that is why he could lie so fluently and without compunction, because he did not care if he was caught, he would just lie some more. And he did not care if someone got hurt because he did not feel it.

14. Mother Nature

Work scene on ceramic vessel,
Cyprus, 2200–1800 BCE

To our enormous surprise, after a couple of weeks, Philip wound up in a rather swish unit at a multi-storey apartment block called Fairways, with a balcony and a view over floodlit tennis courts. Naturally, it was all paid for by Normie, who was still trying to push through the insurance claim from the Big Burglary. The insurers continued to stand their ground and the matter stuttered through a series of court appearances, all of it building up to either a massive payout or, potentially, gaol time for Philip. Mum had it in her head that if Philip and Normie were successful and received a payout, then she deserved a bit of it. At least, that was the excuse she gave us for calling Philip every day, chatting amiably, tittering at his dumb jokes and occasionally trading vile insults with him. Once in a while, we would encounter a shard of splintered glass in the carpet, a little reminder that just a few weeks earlier Philip had hurled pot plants through the windows and threatened to murder us all.

Some nights Philip would stay with us. Some nights he would invite Mum over to his apartment at Fairways and she would take at least one of her children with her as a kind of human shield. John never went and Philip never pressed him to. John was almost the same height as Philip by now. His voice had broken, he was starting to shave, and Philip had become wary of him. Not of me though. I was still a skinny kid.

They say that birds of a feather flock together. Get yourself a lazy, criminal, violent, alcoholic stepfather and you will meet a sweeping array of truly monumental losers. It amazes me that although I grew up rubbing shoulders with these drunks and failed criminals, not one of them ever took me aside and said, 'Listen son, take a good long look at me and learn from my mistakes. Be smart, get a job, settle down, live an honest and clean life.' Not one of them ever said that because they all thought of themselves as remarkable people with stellar IQs. Vanity is often concentrated in those who have the least to boast about.

And all of these men loved barbecues, or gathering for the Melbourne Cup or a grand final, or any other social pretext for putting away a skinful of booze and ignoring their wives and children. Because at the heart of it all, the people that we mixed with at this time were selfish, and selfishness so often ends with cruelty. It rarely ends with friendship, which was reflected in how often the losers in our orbit owed money to each other. This abuse of the fraternity's code happened all the time but was taken very personally.

We were to witness this firsthand one morning at Fairways. Sophie and I had both stayed the night and Philip offered to drive us to school, which was a dodgy proposition because at the time he was driving a gorgeous gold-coloured, American-made and imported Oldsmobile that had no brakes. Well, it had brakes, but you could not drive it at above forty kilometres per hour and you had to stop by pumping the brake pedal ten or twenty times to bring the beast to a gentle stop. It took real skill and an unbelievable level of anticipatory driving. Fifty metres before pulling into our driveway Philip would have to start pumping the brake, left leg going like the clappers, easing the car to a safe turning speed, all the while trying to look completely normal from the waist up. Smiling at neighbours. Waving. Left leg pumping.

Anyway, on this morning, Philip walked with us to the Fairways carpark and when we got to the Oldsmobile we found a dead, fat, ginger cat flopped across the windshield with its head caved in. And here is the kicker: we knew that it was a message from someone who Philip owed money to – probably the man who had recently hit him with a walking stick – but he owed money to so many people that he was not quite sure which one it was. So, waste of a good cat. After Mum (*Mum!*) had taken the corpse off the bonnet and dumped it in a big bin, Sophie and I just went to school in that dodgy Oldsmobile, little kittycat footprints on its rooftop.

Cats have been bringing joy to humans for 9500 years, a poor second to dogs though, who have been getting their ears scratched by humans for at least 23,000 years, probably much longer. Humans have always had an ambiguous relationship with nature, partly because we eat lots of it, and lots of it can kill us. When I was a young archaeologist, I lived for four months in a tiny village in central Cyprus while I swung a pick on the site of a prehistoric Bronze Age settlement some 4200 years old. We found a number of ceramic bulls, just two or three centimetres tall, modelled at a time soon after the introduction of cattle to the island. What a difference they must have made to the people there. Cattle for meat and milk, muscle to pull a plough, hides for leather shoes. What joy! But it is hard to know what the makers of those little figurines were thinking. Were they depicting nature or chattels? The people of prehistoric Cyprus also fashioned birds, rabbits, sheep, pigs and deer out of clay. They liked animals well enough, but did the animals bring them joy as 'nature' or as the main course?

There is just enough, though, in prehistoric art to suggest that people – some anyway – derived non-gastronomic joy from the natural world. There are wavy underwater seaweed gardens in Minoan art from Crete, and broad-petalled flowers in the Neolithic art of Anatolia. And what could be behind the 14,000-year-old bison of La Madeleine but a kind of reverence for a part of the natural world? The person who created this masterpiece in what is now southwest France had *observed* the creature, its powerful chest and muscular hindlegs, its arcing horns and shaggy beard, and did so with deep respect.

At the end of that four-month project on Cyprus I was left behind to pack up the equipment and return the keys.

The morning after everyone else had left I was overwhelmed by the gentle quietness of the village, the occasional tolling church bell, a bleating goat, the shuffling footsteps of an elderly yaya. I went for a stroll down narrow lanes to the edge of the village, and as I turned the last corner past a mudbrick house in the old style, making for the terraced hillsides, I walked into a flock of sparrows hurtling towards me at eye level. They were as surprised to see me as I was them, an unexpected murmuration, as some peeled off to the left, others to the right, 200 tiny beating hearts, 400 little thumping wings, dividing past my ears and whirring off out of my sight and hearing. It thrilled me to have come face to face with a little bit of nature.

And Philip? He couldn't have cared less about that dead cat. We lived at this time in a cramped urban environment that was already starting to get cluttered by high-rise buildings. We were occasionally swooped by a magpie but were otherwise surrounded by concrete. The surf was 200 metres away but the closest we got to nature was the big brown cockroaches infesting our pantry. This was Philip's preferred environment, seedy and urban.

Incredibly, as I have noted, we had a dog through all of the dislocations and disruptions of our time with Philip. Shandy – a floppy-eared, placid, patient, dopey, shaggy golden retriever – had been given to me as a puppy on my eleventh birthday. He had followed us from house to house in Canberra and on the Gold Coast, his tail always wagging excitedly as we dragged him from pillar to post, long-suffering, uncomplaining and unquestioning. He was full of affection and clumsy gentleness, and incapable of understanding a single command. Even the easy one – 'Sit!' – was tough for him, although to be fair his tail was usually wagging so furiously that sitting was difficult. His tail only stopped wagging when Philip was drunk. When that happened, Shandy would slink into a corner watchfully, ears down. More than any of us, Shandy understood Philip's baser animal instincts. And Shandy had felt Philip's irrational drunken wrath. He had been beaten, kicked and punched by my stepfather. When Philip threw us out of the house in Sorrento, Shandy stayed behind. By the time Philip was back on the scene at Broadbeach, I asked after him and was told that Shandy had been given to a farmer on the north coast of New South Wales who owned a huge property where he could run and play and explore. I didn't believe him. Instead, I imagined Shandy in a cage at the RSPCA, a needle, his tail wagging excitedly, and then ceasing to wag.

*

We can be certain that human company has always brought people the most joy, even though it may be difficult to find evidence of it in prehistoric art. Of course, there is the music and dancing which speak eloquently for firm and affirming friendship. And what is the point of a gaming board or a feast if not a bit of chummy conversation between moves, and laughter between courses? A quiet conversation between loving friends is hard to reproduce with wet clay or by applying pigment to the surface of an Ice Age wall, but take the scene modelled in clay on the exterior of a vessel from prehistoric Bronze Age Cyprus that depicts (as part of a more complex scene) a woman breastfeeding her infant while a line of three women behind her grind grain, leaning into the task, and three others stand around a deep mortar as they pound the grain with a pestle. A tedious and exhausting process. Archaeologists have analysed the scene, and others like it, from the perspective of trade, crop yields and industry. But we must not forget that as these women toiled over their grinding stones, they were certainly sharing stories about their husbands, giggling at bad jokes, commiserating over the loss of loved ones, celebrating newborns. These exchanges brought joy and meaning to their lives. They were bonding and sharing, as friends do.

In Broadbeach, we had nobody to turn to. Our association with Philip had stripped us of friends and the comfort and pleasure that they can bring. They peeled off, wisely avoiding the catastrophe that had engulfed us and the man who was responsible for it. In Philip's case, when friendships turned bad, the cat bought it.

The day after the dead cat was found on the bonnet of our car, Philip thought he would make it up to us by going into town and getting bashed up by a bouncer. That was good of him. It cheered me no end. And the day after that was his forty-fifth birthday. Philip's birthday was a big deal to him. Other people's birthdays, not so much. He launched himself bodily into a month-long binge. He was not sober for four weeks, not for one minute of one day. Some nights he would stay in his unit at Fairways and some nights he would roll through our door drunk and stay the night. Sometimes he was giggly and happy, but often he was mirthless and surly. He would stake his claim at the dining table, three paces from the lounge that I slept on, and he would silently stew. We had no television to turn down, but our conversation ceased in case somebody said something that would set him off. Mum would flit around our tiny kitchen nervously, appeasing him with baked beans and scrambled eggs with bacon, while her children just sat there reading books or staring out the window, the room humming with tension.

The circuit-breaker came from an unexpected quarter. Normie could see his Big Burglary investment going down the toilet while his main man poisoned himself with toxic levels of alcohol. One day in the late morning, while we sat quietly in our loungeroom, fearful of waking the drunken stepfather asleep in the bedroom, Normie appeared at the front door of our unit, one that he had never been to before, and walked in without knocking. A big man, he filled the tiny loungeroom. Taking in the pathetic scene (three desperately poor kids and their mother) even he paused for a moment with something that may have approximated embarrassment or shame. 'Where's Philip?' he growled. We pointed to the door of his/Mum's/Sophie's bedroom and he marched in. Normie was not someone to mess with. He was known to have hurt people, and perhaps more frighteningly, was known to have paid others to hurt people for him. I heard Normie ordering Philip to get up and then, with utter disgust, he watched as Philip dragged himself out of bed to dress. Normie snarled contemptuously, 'You lazy bum...', and then he strode out before Philip had finished dressing, and without acknowledging us as he departed. A minute later, Philip scrambled out after him, doing up his belt, looking meek, smiling weakly. Even in his sozzled state he knew how pathetic he looked, this time in the eyes of a known thug, and it may even have been dawning on him that while he could beat my mother from time to time, when it came to another man, he was nothing but a chickenshit.

We did not hear from Philip for three days. I gloried in it, but Mum was worried, so she went to the Gold Coast races on the Saturday knowing that Philip (if he was alive) would be there. He was, and he was inexplicably cashed up, but when Mum approached him and asked for money for dinner, he told her to fuck off. She poured a glass of brandy over his head (a trend was emerging) and stormed off leaving Philip fuming and his mates chortling at him. When Mum came home, she and I walked the forty-five minutes to Fairways – we had no car – and used the spare key to break in. Our objective was primitive and basic: steal what could be sold for money to cover our dinner. As it turned out, there was not much to steal. Bizarrely, I recall walking home again carrying a volume from the Zondervan encyclopaedic bible series!

A few days later, they threw Philip out of Fairways and he moved in with another big drinker named Harry. Harry was on the slippery slope to oblivion, but nevertheless, he carried himself with a certain dignity and had something of a gentlemanly bearing, including rounded vowels and a knack for a witty one-liner. These things all suggested that

Harry could have been something a little better if he had not been cursed with a taste for the drink. One afternoon around this time Philip brought Harry over to our unit to introduce him to us. They had been cruising the length of the Gold Coast beach strip that day, visiting surf clubs where they sold cheap fluffy toys to middle-aged men looking for forgiveness from wives and children. Being nature lovers, the toys were a mix of stuffed cows, horses, penguins and teddy bears. Naturally, both Philip and Harry were very drunk. I can see them even now, their pitifulness enhanced by the fact that within five minutes of arriving Harry had slipped off the lounge and sat in a bowl of warm water that my mother had been soaking her feet in as part of her latest beauty regime. It took him a long time to notice and even longer to get to his feet. I thought of him as a fool. Another one. I watched him walk with a sway out the door with Philip, to drink-drive home in his wet trousers, with a green stuffed dinosaur under his arm, legs bowed to minimise chafing.

15. Wasters

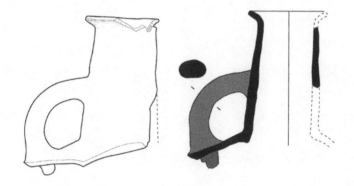

Fragmentary Prehistoric Bronze Age vessel,
Cyprus, c1800 BCE

In prehistory, making pottery was challenging. The kilns were usually rudimentary, sometimes nothing more than a bonfire with the unfired clay vessels stacked in the centre. It was difficult to get the temperature right. If a brisk wind picked up when the fire had begun, the temperatures might soar and hours of toil – collecting the clay, levigating it, slaking it, shaping the pots – would be for nought. Exposed to a steady and unbearable rise in temperature, the vessels would warp and shatter. When that happened, archaeologists find twisted, super-heated fragments of pottery discarded in ashy deposits. The broken pieces that couldn't bear the rising temperatures are called wasters.

Two weeks after we had raided Philip's Fairways apartment, he came by in a bad mood, the scary kind. Mum was sipping a cup of tea, preparing for bed, when Philip walked in, his dark eyes darting. He wanted a drink and his wife was coming with him. Mum was too scared to argue. We all sensed the change in him and the seething incomprehensible rage. She hastened to the bedroom to put on a dress while Philip sat silently brooding in the loungeroom in the company of his three stepchildren. Nobody spoke as the minutes passed in agonising tension. What must he have been thinking? What must it feel like to have to confront your own failings and cruelties so often? How must it feel to sit with three children who had been born into a nice house and who now lived in a shithole because of you?

Mum and Philip left together and I had a bad feeling. John, Sophie and I sat watching television as the minutes ticked away, the three of us cramped in the dingy loungeroom, pale faces outstaring the flickering screen. It was late evening but warm. Our neighbours, my school friends, the churchgoers, the holidaymakers, our alienated friends and family had no idea. Our anxiety at these times was beyond their comprehension. We closed the door. We waited. We spoke in low murmurs. We didn't dress for bed, even as it grew late. An hour passed. Then another. When we heard a car door slam, we all looked up, someone turned the television down. Mum put the key in the door and walked in, alone.

In some noisy wine bar, surrounded by fun seekers, Mum and Philip had run into Harry, and when Philip swore at Mum and threatened her, Harry had risen to his feet in indignation and beaten the shit out of Philip. It turns out that there was more to Harry than met the eye. Mum left when the bouncers intervened and came home to her children. I recall these events with amazement and all these years later still feel the raised heartbeat, the flush of adrenaline and the fatigue that followed a sense of relief. It was coming though – we knew it – when all that adrenaline would not be wasted.

And that television? Mum had hocked her rings for it, the ones that she had owned since before her time with Philip. All that sentimentality and romance, all those memories, flogged to some hardnosed pawn broker on the Gold Coast. She never saw those rings again, but we got the television out of it. Philip walked in on the first night we watched it and paused briefly, saying nothing. For a moment I feared that he would smash the screen, but it was always more likely that he would sell it. He made no comment and neither did we, and we were still watching that television years later. But the downward spiral for Philip continued. Less than two weeks after Harry had beaten Philip up and thrown him out, he slouched into our unit one evening and demanded a bed to sleep in.

Suffice to say, he was not especially welcome at the time so when he came in and demanded the bed, Mum ordered him out. Instead of shame, embarrassment and humiliation Philip puffed out his chest and stood his ground. Holding Mum's eye coolly, he walked into Mum's bedroom, kicked off his shoes, peeled off his shirt and shucked off his pants. Crawling into bed he drew the bedspread up over himself and refused point blank to leave. 'I can't go,' he said. 'I'm naked.'

Mum called us into the bedroom and her three children stood at the foot of the bed while she berated her husband, sheets drawn up to his chinny-chin-chin. Get out. Nope. Out! Nope! Mum grabbed the bedspread and started yanking. He held on like a six-year-old but regathering his composure he warned, 'I have no clothes on and there are women present.' There was a little breather as Sophie was ordered to leave the room and then the tug of war started again with John and I watching. Then Philip just gave up with a casual hands-behind-the-head well-you-asked-for-it nonchalance and the covers came off leaving him lying starkers on the bed with his two teenaged stepsons looking at him in horror. He tried to play it cool at first, just lay there, but after a few excruciating seconds Philip's right hand slid down his flank and over to his manhood. And so, what does one do when standing over a bed looking at a naked stepfather? You snigger at him. In several years of turning points, this was the irrecoverable one, one from which Philip could never come back, the man unmanned, naked and a fool. I had always been scared of him but in that instant, in my mind he became a truly pathetic figure.

*

I have wondered, from time to time, what a beat-up second-hand kid's bike was worth when I was fourteen years old. Somehow, I had managed to hang on to my old banger through the evictions and dislocations of my life with Philip, always managing to reclaim it when our hoard of belongings was eventually returned to us. That is what being poor is: hanging on to beat up things longer than everybody else, if you can get your hands on them in the first place. The bike was a reminder of pre-Philip days, when Mum could afford to buy us bicycles, but it showed its age. The paint was chipping off, the brakes squeaked, and on hot days the plastic seat would scald your bum. But it was my only ticket to freedom in some respects and allowed me to independently get to school and back, saving me an hour of walking each day.

Not long after we moved into the Broadbeach unit Philip sold my bike. So instead, every afternoon as I trudged home, I had to look on as another kid from my school would swish by me on *my* bicycle. Over beers in some pub, Philip had sold my bicycle to the kid's father. The boy was classy and touchingly adult about it. We did not know each other, but he knew where the bike had come from. One hot afternoon he stopped for no reason other than to say hello, two teenagers chatting, one on a bike looking politely guilty and one walking home. We never spoke again, but sometimes that boy would give a little wave as he scooted past me, heading for his home, while I shouldered my school bag and made for mine. I suppose I could have been resentful, but it was not the kid's fault. It was Philip's fault. So, how much did Philip get for that crappy old bike? My guess is that he got enough for a chicken parmigiana and a few beers. I walked five hours every week to go to school so that Philip could get drunk *once*.

Philip's mind was not calibrated for such calculations. Philip was an alcoholic. *That* is what he was. That is *all* that he was. There was no room for anything else except, maybe, gambling and women. He laughed at the hard work and dedication of other people, saw no point to it. He resented talent in others. There was a tiny part of his heart that was a little warmer, where he stored ill-defined feelings for his biological daughters. Sometimes he even remembered to call them on their birthdays. But his three stepchildren, me included, were nothing to him. We were never anything but an inconvenience. Every molecule of his body was dedicated to acquiring and consuming alcohol, and to gratifying his personal desires.

The Scythians were an ancient people who inhabited the vast Eurasian steppes in the fifth century BCE – the unforgiving plains of what is now southern Russia and its surrounds. They were hardy and ferocious nomads, and a source of endless fascination for the ancient Greeks who regarded them with a mix of horror and fear. The Greek historian, Herodotus, spent time with them some 2450 years ago and recorded some of their more unusual habits, not least their custom of scalping enemies killed in battle and turning the skin into handy napkins that they wore around their necks. They also liked to cut off the top of the poor victim's cranium and make a cup out of it. When milking their cattle – so the Scythians informed the keen ethnographer Herodotus – they would blow air into the cow's bottom using a straw fashioned out of bone, to make the milk come out more quickly, which suggests to me that they may have had a sense of humour after all. I imagine a group of Scythians on a windswept steppe laughing about the time they tricked a gullible Greek into sticking a straw into a bemused cow's bum and giving it a good blow. Or maybe they really did do that when milking their cows. If so, the blowing-into-a-cow's-bum-with-a-straw job is one of the less appealing career choices in recorded ancient history, maybe even pipping the palace armpit-plucker noted in Minoan records over 3000 years ago.

Herodotus also describes the Scythians building little tents out of felt, which they would sit inside, and where they would throw hemp seeds onto hot stones. They would then breathe in the smoke from the burning seeds and, as Herodotus describes it, howl with pleasure. Little wonder. They were high as kites.

Humans have been intoxicating themselves for thousands of years. Opium, marijuana, magic mushrooms, peyote, wine and beer. Most of these things were easy to find or make but beer – my stepfather's drug of choice – was more difficult than most. To brew beer it is necessary to break down the starches in grain to make the fermentable sugars, and it so happens that an excellent enzyme for that purpose is found in human saliva. So, in traditional cultures around the world and, it seems, parts of prehistoric Europe and the Middle East, people would gather around pots of barley in the evening and gob in them – all part of the beer-making process – and afterwards they would get drunk. You have got to really love a beer buzz to drink a brew fermented with someone else's saliva. But humans like the buzz. It brings us joy, even though some of us get addicted. Joy for some. Pain for others. And some people like it so much that they will put intoxicants above friends and family. That was Philip.

So, what are the after-effects for the victims? What are the ripples on the outer edge of the expanding circles? What is the dull ache that lingers in the children long after the other symptoms have passed? What remains after you have grown up and left behind a violent, boozy and impoverished household? You carry things with you.

Firstly, there is wariness and bewilderment. In your teens and twenties, you circle big drunk men in pubs with their deep voices and rough-and-tumble, you keep a low profile when the shouting starts, you tip-toe around the workplace bully, sometimes you come awfully close to demeaning yourself. And you hate yourself for that but having seen the results of 'making trouble' for violent people who are stronger than you are, you think twice, and think again. Not everyone is a superhero. And not everyone can be Gandhi. If you have never seen a man punch a woman, you can begin to think that it could never really happen. That makes some people bold, where all your experience tells *you* to be afraid. It means raised voices can tighten your stomach, send your heart pounding and make your mouth run dry.

Secondly, there is resentment and diminished opportunity. Everyone seems rich, everyone seems luckier than you, even ordinary people raised in unremarkable suburban houses seem ridiculously well placed. They can afford to take a risk, because if they fail they have a safety net to fall elegantly and confidently back into – a loving family, accumulated savings. Through my twenties, even into my thirties, every tiny investment in the future felt like the last roll of the dice. No safety net. Just a looming chasm.

It takes time to repair yourself. All the bits of you that are supposed to be sharp are worn down and smoothed by the ebb and flow of events that you lived through, and all those bits that are supposed to be smooth are brittle and serrated. In my case, I have always been a bad read: having been raised by a monster, I have often fallen into the trap of thinking that anybody who falls short of being a monster must be alright. But people can be monstrous without being as bad as Philip was.

And thirdly, there is the intolerance. I know that alcoholism is a disease but here is how it is for the victims of violent alcoholics: every beer is a decision. And every time the decision to drink alcohol is taken, a certain thought process is followed – I can hurt my family or I can gratify myself for the next twenty minutes. Living in dire straits, it is difficult to make concessions to the alcoholic's needs, it is much easier and more understandable to make judgements.

In the Broadbeach unit the temperature kept rising.

*

He walks in late at night and sits at the dinner table without saying a word. In the confined space, there is no ignoring him. I can smell the booze. Sickening. But worse is his sense of entitlement, which seeps to every corner of our little unit like an infection. His resentments surface. He wants the television turned off. He wants dinner. He wants beer.

I look at Mum who holds my eye. It is the signal. I walk out of the loungeroom silently, as if I am going to my bedroom, but instead I turn down the short hallway, pass through the bathroom and quietly open the back door. I slip out in bare feet, leap the patch of bindi-eye near the bins and sprint the length of our block of units to Surf Parade, which is still warm from the hot day, but quiet now and empty. Turning left, I run the 100 metres to the Broadbeach Police Station. The front steps are a cold-white colour, stark under bright fluorescent lights that moths throw themselves at with fleshy thwacks. I take the stairs two at a time and run into the foyer where a twenty-something copper in a blue uniform is standing behind a wide counter, looking bored. I go to him and tell him breathlessly: 'We live just down the road, my stepfather is drunk and violent, and he is going to hit my mum.' My skinny legs are trembling. The copper listens at first, but before I can finish a supercilious smile creeps across his face. He calls over his shoulder: 'Hey Steve. This kid says his father's going to beat his mum up.'

Another twenty-something in uniform walks out from behind a partition. Two big men. 'Oh, is he now?' replies Steve. Then to me, 'Well maybe you should run on home then.'

They both start laughing and as the laughter ebbs away the first one says, 'What's your address?' He listens as I answer but he doesn't write anything down, then he tells me to go home. 'We might send someone by a bit later.'

I walk down the stairs past the flapping moths, out onto the warm footpath and trot home in the humid stillness of a Queensland summer evening. I jump the bindi-eye, slip back in through the back door, and walk into the living room to find Philip hunched over the dinner table eating bubble-and-squeak. Mum looks up at me and I shake my head.

Nobody comes.

Two weeks later he fractures her cheek.

All these years later I am sitting here still wondering what it was that I said that night that was so funny.

*

It had to end. But *how* did it end? Book I of *The Iliad* ends when Hephaestus recalls for his mother the time that Zeus hurled him off Olympus. After he counsels her to stop resisting, she retires to the marriage bed and meekly lies down beside her husband, her abuser. There was no ending for Hera. I always felt that our ending had to feel like revenge. It had to be retributive. We were lucky. For many victims of violent men, there is no happy ending.

It is late evening and dark. John, Sophie and I are in the loungeroom watching the television bought with the proceeds of my mother's hocked jewellery. I can hear Mum in the bedroom. She's just had a shower and is settling down for the night. She will put curlers in her wet hair, wrap her head in a red nylon scarf and go to sleep beside my sister in the same double bed. She's humming to herself. Crickets are whirring outside. Things are pretty close to normal. The front door is open.

My stepfather walks in like he owns the place, like he pays the rent, like he belongs here. He walks in like he feeds and clothes us. He walks in like a man who knows he won't be challenged. He walks in with anger in his eye. We sit up straighter, but we don't ask him what he thinks he's doing. We know better by now.

He nods a perfunctory hello at us and passes directly into Mum's room. He wants a drink. We have been here before. There can only be one result. Mum raises a small protest: 'I can't go out with curlers in my hair.' But he won't take no for an answer, so she tucks the loose hair under the edges of her scarf and puts on a dress. Philip waits. We all do.

'We won't be long kids,' she tells us as she emerges from the bedroom. As they walk out, we say goodbye. We watch them go and turn our attention back to the TV. We do not close the front door.

They are gone for maybe two hours. When they return we hear the car pull up in the driveway and the car doors slamming closed, one after the other, then Mum's high heels clacking and scraping down the concrete towards the front door. This must be unremarkable in most families – the car doors closing and the footsteps. In most families the children know what to expect: Mum and Dad strolling in, maybe a kiss goodnight, light-hearted teasing and tickles. But we are all on edge.

I am sitting with a book on my lap when she comes in. I glance up. My god! Her eye is already swollen. It's pink and tender and puffing into a slit. She looks wild. A distressed animal. A cornered cat. A whipped dog. There's something in her eye that's frightening. Hysteria. Fear. Her hair is falling out from under the scarf, her curlers have been shaken loose, her eyes roll in her head. This image I carry with me: she rests one hand on the doorknob, gestures with the other. Wordless. Unable to speak. She swallows and says to us at last: 'Look what he's done to me!'

Then Philip walks in, brushing past her, the big man, huge smile on his face. Giggling.

Things happened very quickly. John was on his feet. I stood up. A little knot of tension, atoms repelling and attracting. It had been building to this for years. Five people in a tiny loungeroom, a fraction of a second, time congealing, raised voices.

I heard my mother plead: 'Leave him alone.'

I heard Philip snarl: 'He thinks he's a man. Let him stand up for himself.'

As he advanced on my brother, Mum stepped aside. John stood his ground, a schoolboy not quite seventeen years old. He had snatched up a piece of timber dowelling that we used to slide into the window tracks as a substitute for a broken lock. Philip didn't see it and he prowled forward with his fists up, determined to put John in his place. But the world turns. Kids grow up. They learn and become wise. They watch and become brave and hateful.

John brought down the piece of dowelling on Philip's head with all his strength and it splintered into two pieces, stunning Philip and leaving John holding a sharpened piece of timber dowelling in his hand, the length of a knife. He swung at Philip's body two, three, four times, using it like a long blade, stabbing down from above his shoulder and up from his waist. The bully was screaming for help as the point scraped across his chest, and he bent forward, protecting the top of his head with his hands. At one point he tried to stand and John, tossing aside the timber, landed a punch on the side of Philip's head near the temple. Then another.

Philip was roaring and Mum was screaming hysterically. I heard her shriek, 'Kill him!' As Philip tried to unfurl himself, I leapt onto him. I felt the back of his hot head on my sternum as I wrapped my arms around his torso and I tried to drag him down. I remember thinking that he might bite me and as he drew himself up, he brought me with him, a skinny teenager and no great threat or impediment. I slipped down and away in the one motion and John landed a couple more blows. Crack. Crack. Even my sister was in there briefly, darting in once to slap and kick him. He roiled about. Finally *he* was the trapped animal. Another punch. More screaming.

It was mayhem, there was shouting and sobs, and then suddenly there was stillness. Everyone stepped back, breathing deeply, and Philip was left cowering in the middle of the room, a full-grown man, surrounded by a woman and her three children, swaying a little, stupid from the blows and the booze, as we entered the most dangerous five seconds of my life. In that moment, if he had wanted to, Philip could have ended it all. A wild, violent, hate-filled psychopath, he had the strength and means to damage us, even to kill us, but his head was throbbing, the booze was making him wobbly, his addled mind just wasn't up to murder. We regarded each other, panting like animals.

And then another strange thing: Philip spied an electric shaver on the credenza. It was not his, but he picked it up possessively and growled, 'I'm leaving.' So far as us kids were concerned, he was welcome to the shaver, but Mum wasn't having it. She snatched at it, got a hand to it and there was a wrestling match. John shouted, 'Give him the fucking shaver, Mum.' But she held on for dear life, got the better of him, snatched it out of his hand and held the trophy to her chest. Another little victory.

Philip swayed, feeling his head for blood, then walked to the door, boiling with frustration, mad with confusion, sobbing. He paused at the threshold he had abused so many times and crossed it. Mum ran forward and slammed the door closed behind him and I rushed after her and locked it.

And then, I heard the last words that my stepfather ever uttered directly to me, ringing out of the night-time darkness, angry and whimpering through the door closed on his back: 'You can all go and get fucked!'

*

The months that followed felt like the eye of a storm. We learned that Philip was telling people that John had attacked him with a knife and that he was going to take it to the police. Mercifully, Mum made no effort to find Philip, and incredibly, after the beating, Mum went to the police and reported him for assault. They took down her details, filed the doctor's report and the X-rays of her fractured cheek, took photos of her bruised and swollen face. And they assured her that if Philip ever crossed paths with the police again, even for something as trivial as a parking ticket, it would all appear on their system and he would be charged. He was in court a few times after that that we know of, for other matters. No charges were ever pressed by them for something as paltry as domestic violence.

We heard nothing from Philip himself, a bully nursing his wounds. But then three months later, just short of my fifteenth birthday and as another Christmas approached, the tension increased. In the heat of summer, we kept the front door closed and locked. On Christmas eve, after we had watched Carols by Candlelight on the telly and turned out the lights, I was dozing off on the lounge/my bed when there came a soft knock at the door. My head was about three metres from it, under an open window. I could hear his breathing, then Philip's voice, soft but clear, as he called out my mother's name. I didn't answer, but I heard Mum get up and I watched as she walked to the door and opened it. The eagles linking talons and spiralling to earth together?

There was a short, muffled conversation, Philip's wheedling voice, then he handed Mum $200 and he left. Mum closed the door gently, locked it and returned to her bed. I lay on my side with my eyes closed and drifted off to sleep. This time – no really, this time – it felt over.

Perhaps Mum was thinking about this: a couple of days earlier, a different man had appeared at our door carrying a box full of packages wrapped in plain brown paper. He told us that he was from Lifeline or the Smith Family or the Salvation Army (I can't remember). He checked that he had the right address and then with a smile he placed the box at the door. He wished us 'Merry Christmas' and departed with a cheery wave.

We opened the box and pored over the packages, incredulous. Each one had a little label on it wishing us a Merry Christmas, together with an impersonal handwritten note: *For a boy aged twelve to fourteen,* or *Girl's present aged eight to twelve.* They were Christmas presents, donated by kindly people, for children in need. We never worked out who told them about us but there were plenty of people who had seen the shit we were in. We were officially some of the poorest kids in the city. Literally charity cases. But I was not too proud to take my new, handmade kite outside and fly it high above our unit on Christmas Day. It is still the loveliest Christmas present that I have ever received, from somebody I had never met and who I have never been able to thank.

16. The Dying Beast

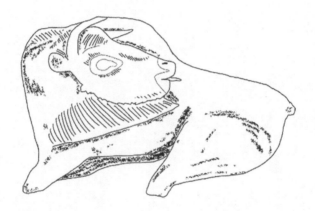

Bison licking its flank, La Madeleine,
France, c13,000 BCE

There were still the last nervous twitches of the dying beast that was Mum's marriage to Philip. As the new year began, there remained the sense that we were being watched. I would glance warily over my shoulder on the walk to and from school every day. The ring of the phone would startle us. And it rang a lot, only for us to hear silence or, worse, shallow breathing on the end of the line when we answered. We were anxious. Also, we were poor, terribly poor. With schoolbooks, school uniforms and dinner to buy, Mum went back to one of those happy-clappy churches that we had attended with Philip. Out of shame, she saved her pleas for the carpark, away from prying eyes, where she asked the pastor's son for money to help us get back on our feet. The soul-destroying shame! He gave us $20. We bought a takeaway chicken, chips and coleslaw for dinner with it. A few days later the church's pastor phoned to see how we were, and to compound our indignity, to give Mum a little lecture on how it is that the Lord helps those who help themselves instead of those who rely on charity. He wouldn't be giving us any more money, he counselled. At the time, this man was living with his whole family in a Gold Coast mansion donated to his church by a wealthy Korean businessman. Charity means different things to different people.

Around this time we drove down to Canberra in our beat-up, twenty-year-old car to watch my father remarry. We were so good at it by now – standing there, smiling politely, looking like we were a happy, relatively normal family. Nobody would have guessed that we were penniless, broken and confused. Dad seemed happy with his new wife, but we hadn't seen him for a couple of years and he was beginning to seem like an acquaintance to me. He told us that he had sent us Christmas presents a few weeks before, but they had been returned with a note saying that we had moved to Western Australia. He was pleased that we could make it to the wedding. After it, we piled back into the car and returned to Surfers Paradise, waving cheerily at cousins and aunts and uncles as we left.

We still had not heard anything from Philip. I was hoping that he was at the bottom of the Pacific Ocean with rocks in his boots, courtesy of Normie, but Mum still couldn't let go. Rather than celebrate, she reported Philip to the police as a missing person. Then the beat-up old car that we were driving was stolen, which we figured – naturally – was Philip's doing. Mum took John to Normie's little unit so that we could demand it back. John stood at Normie's front door – Normie, the known violent criminal, convicted mobster, ex-jailbird – and told him that he wanted the car back or he would go to the police about the Big Burglary.

Normie rose to his feet and said nothing, slipped his door keys into his pocket and walked John down the front stairs and across the street to a public phone booth. He dialled a number, handed the phone to John and walked off. Philip was on the other end of the line. He denied any knowledge of the theft of our car. He was in New Zealand.

Two weeks later, our abandoned car showed up in a beachside carpark. It probably was not Philip, but it started him to thinking, because a couple of weeks later he sent Mum a telegram asking her to call him. Naturally, we all begged her not to call him back. Life was slowly getting back to normal as we were finding some stability again. John had started his final year of high school. I was in Grade 10 and Sophie was in Grade 8. There was light at the end of the tunnel. There was potential. But Mum did call him, of course. I do not know what she expected to hear, but what she got was a drunk, giggling Philip introducing her to his new girlfriend who said she 'was really sorry' about the telegram. Mum told her: 'You have my sympathies.' Recalling the anonymous letter of warning all those years earlier, Mum also warned the woman that Philip was a violent conman. When the woman grew agitated Philip came back on the phone. He ended the conversation with what he must have taken to be a compliment to Mum: 'You're not a bad bird, are you.'

The spooks lingered. This manifested itself in bizarre ways. Nine months after Philip had knocked on our door that final Christmas Eve, we had another visitor on our doorstep. Shandy, our dopey golden retriever, who I had given up for dead, mysteriously appeared one Saturday evening as the sun was going down. He just emerged out of the twilight, tail wagging and with a perplexed expression on his face. We were gobsmacked. All golden retrievers look alike but this was definitely our crooked-toothed Shandy with a distinctive scar on his snout. He walked in looking confused and embarrassed and submitted to our amazed pats and tickles. After a bit he lay down on our loungeroom floor, between us and the telly, and just went to sleep. He lay there for about two hours, dozing or wagging his tail amiably, while we talked it over. What were we going to do with him in a tiny unit where pets weren't allowed? And how did he get there?

Clearly, Philip was somewhere nearby. Think on that. Really think on it. A violent madman with underworld connections was somewhere nearby, and he had gone to the trouble of finding our old dog on a property in northern New South Wales, putting him in a car, and releasing him near our front door one pleasant evening. Then, he had slinked away. As we talked it over, suddenly, Shandy sat up, ears pricked and trotted out the door, pausing only briefly to look over his shoulder at us. A dog whistle beyond our human hearing. We never saw him again. Philip was messing with our heads.

We also lived in the shadow of the Big Burglary. Of course, the insurance company was very keen to speak with Mum. She knew dates and places and people. In fact, she knew enough for those very shady characters to see her as a serious problem. Inevitably, the Queensland Police invited Mum into an important-looking edifice for a chat. It was an invitation that she could not refuse. The insurance claim was playing itself out before the courts, the insurance company resisting the payout on the understandable grounds that there was insufficient evidence of any of the insured goods ever actually existing, and no evidence that a skint grifter like my stepfather could ever have owned so much lovely expensive stuff.

The Queensland Police were under enormous pressure to investigate the matter as a criminal act of fraud. Perhaps for moral support, but more likely to generate a little sympathy, Mum brought her children with her to the police station. I remember us passing through the foyer of the building where we were signed in. I recall walking past several detectives in a big open-plan office where officers of the law worked to clear our streets of fraudsters and crims. Some of them looked up as we passed, perhaps noticing we three children who were so out of place in that environment. We sat in a fraud squad detective's office where he and a second detective asked Mum questions about the robbery. Where were the insured goods bought? How could you afford them? Where were you on the night of the sixteenth? I sat in silence. Recall: talking is dangerous. At one point, a young detective knocked on the door and asked Mum if she wanted a cup of tea. She did, and he made it for her. Maybe ten people saw us that morning and three spoke to us, all of them detectives, before they were good enough to drive us home in an unmarked police car. An hour later we were sitting in our shitty loungeroom, Mum manically chain smoking and sipping yet another cuppa held with trembling hands, when an enormous thug filled our open doorway, looked down his nose at our loungeroom and declared himself. He was 'a friend of Philip's' whose job it was to make sure that 'everything is alright'. Mum said it was and he fixed her with a threatening stare that lasted several silent seconds, then he turned and left. Simple as that. One short hour after our meeting with the police.

But we were getting better. We started to recover piecemeal. A new phone. A set of saucepans. A new school uniform, from the shop, instead of hand-me-downs. About a year later, a new fold-out bed instead of sleeping on the lounge. I celebrated these things in my diary, things that most people just take for granted, like they were amazing. Imagine diarising that you had acquired a new school shirt.

The losers, conmen, pervs, drunks and users began to recede from our lives and we gradually replaced them with nice people. The storm was passing. The choppy waves were settling. We could see blue sky and hear the chirping of happy birds. I distinctly recall the last time that I felt like we were still in it, still part of that horrible, unsettled place where there is violence and anger and dysfunction. On that final occasion I recognised how close we were, just a little wind change away, from returning to the mess. The whirlpool. An irresistible pull.

One night, about a year later, our phone rang. It was around 3 am. I was sixteen years old and halfway through Grade 11. It was an old friend of Mum's, a woman in tears, hysterical. She begged us to come over. Her husband, Deano, was beating her up. Mum and I walked to the car and drove together to the house in silence. The roads were empty and peaceful. I think that I should have been scared, but I recall being oddly serene. After we pulled up outside, Mum and I walked together up the driveway, a driveway on a nondescript suburban street, kids bikes beside it, resting on their sides. A man's voice could be heard piercing the otherwise still pre-dawn air. I remember being disgusted. Disgusted that I was being dragged back into this kind of life. Mum knocked on the door, and her friend threw it open in despair. 'Oh, thank God. Oh please. Please. Please come in.'

Mum and I crossed the threshold into their suburban bliss. It was a scene that I knew all too well. A frightened woman with a pink mark over her eye, her hands shaking, and the heavy tread of a man approaching. Hearing Mum's female voice, Deano burst out of the hallway, all geared up to shake his fist at another woman. But then he saw me.

When I was sixteen, I was a pale and pasty 180-centimetre-tall beanpole. You could not have imagined a less intimidating person. I was bigger than Deano though, and I saw the strangest thing. I saw Deano stop in his tracks, then he backed away. I was self-aware enough to know how pathetic that was. As the adults gathered in the kitchen to hiss threats and point fingers, I walked to the kitchen table, pulled out a chair, sat, and watched in silence. I regarded the whole thing with contempt. I was over it.

My mother, always up for an argument, started berating Deano, but I had had enough. I was fed up with adults screaming at each other, hitting each other, calling each other names, and then after it had all blown over, kissing, making up while the kids sat in the loungeroom watching cartoons on TV. That night, things were tense but as the growled exchanges played themselves out, Deano kept glancing at me warily and when he did that, I looked him in the eye and said nothing. I think that the look of unconcealed contempt on my face intimidated him. In the end, he picked up his wallet and quietly left.

Mum and I drove home. I sat in the passenger seat as the dawn smudged blue-grey into the sky, knowing with certainty that if I ever married and had a family, I would be a good husband and a gentle father. Two hours later, I dressed wearily and walked to school. Just like normal.

Afterword

The Pink Poodle, Gold Coast, 1967

John, Sophie and I graduated from Merrimac State High School in 1984, 1986 and 1988 respectively. As each of us graduated, we departed the Gold Coast for good. None of us has ever returned to live there. For us, it is a sad place.

John studied law, travelled the world, and is a litigation partner at a law firm in Brisbane. He has won human rights awards for his legal representation of Australians languishing in foreign prisons. He is married with three children. He is a great husband and an excellent father. It has been a long time since he snatched up a boomerang and stared down our stepfather, and almost as long since he hit him with a piece of timber dowelling. John has always been the responsible one.

Sophie studied Occupational Therapy and moved to London where she became a senior practitioner in the National Health Service. She is married with three children. Her relationship with my mother was always fraught, irreparably damaged by our years with Philip. Nevertheless, when Mum was eighty-two years old and dying, Sophie jumped on the first available plane back from the UK to be with her. A couple of hours after her arrival, Sophie and I sat on either side of Mum's bed, with Mum in a deep sleep between us. We were engaged in quiet conversation when Mum stirred and uttered her final words to us, 'For Christ's sake,' she said, 'would you two shut up!' Sophie reached out and rested her hand on Mum's and softly reassured her. Mum went back to sleep. And slept.

Dad reconnected with his children later in life but there was never a strong bond there, which hurt us all. I would occasionally meet him for coffee or brunch, skirting the big issues. It wasn't really fatherhood. He told us that he bore no ill-will towards Mum, which may have been big of him. Or maybe not. If he did something awful that caused his marriage break-up with Mum (an affair?) we will never know. Dad ended up living in a caravan on Bribie Island, but in his final two years of life he was in a nursing home, where he made many friends. Bizarrely, and without anybody planning it, after many years and 1000 kilometres apart he ended up in the same nursing home as my mother, but a couple of years before she moved in. Standing a few metres from my mother's room, you could look out the window at the bedroom that my father had occupied two years before. He died aged seventy-nine.

Mum and Nana were estranged, reconciled, estranged and reconciled through the twenty years after Philip left. Nana died in a nursing home aged eighty-seven. She was very, very small. When I cleaned out her house at Captains Flat I found a bag containing every letter that Mum had ever sent her, starting with the week after Mum moved out of the family home when she was twenty-one.

The Big Burglary was in and out of the courts for two or three years but finally, in 1986, the Supreme Court of Queensland threw the insurance claim out. Philip had failed to show up at a crucial court hearing and the exasperated judge observed that he could see 'no reason to take a lenient view' of Philip's no-show. We were told that had he shown up, he would have been arrested. It was all a phenomenal waste of time.

We don't really know what became of Philip. We understand that he moved to New Zealand and remarried. Someone told us that he and his wife ran a teahouse in a small town for a while. I find it hard to imagine that he dried out, but stranger things have happened. We have since learned that Philip lived into his late seventies. I have not forgiven him.

After I finished school, I studied Arts and Law at the University of Queensland. My first lecture on my first day of university was in ancient history and archaeology, and it was about the Minoans of ancient Crete. The lecturer quoted Aristotle and Thucydides and talked of Arthur Evans and Heinrich Schliemann and I was entranced. I walked out knowing what I wanted to be when I grew up. I finished my law degree and worked in a law firm for a couple of years, but I then put on a backpack and never returned. I obtained a PhD in the archaeology of Cyprus and have dedicated my professional life to archaeology and cultural heritage management. I am happily married and have a lovely son.

And Mum. There was Mum.

After Philip left, she was crippled by nervous stress, prone to fantasies and wild schemes, a victim of paranoia, an arch-manipulator, sometimes needy and sometimes venomous. A few years after the final showdown, Mum was medicated for depression and many years later she was diagnosed with Post Traumatic Stress Disorder. There were other things there that we will never be able to put a name to. And then a couple of years after we had thrown Philip out, Mum started to complain of numbness in her legs and pain in her back, and when I was twenty, she was diagnosed with multiple sclerosis, the same illness that had killed her brother so cruelly. For years she was all but bedbound, but she stabilised and went into a partial remission. She fought it for the rest of her life. Mum saved up and bought a car. She enrolled at university, and the woman who never went to high school obtained a Bachelor of Arts, winning an award for excellence in literature. In her early seventies, she met a man and formed a strong friendship with him. He was kind to her. They went on cruises and package holidays together, all over the world.

When I was a child, my mother exposed me to awful people and dangerous situations. I don't know why. I don't think she knew why either. But Mum loved me fiercely. Our relationship to the very day she died laboured under the weight of unspoken resentment. But she did love me.

And so, when I feel myself rushing to judgement, I try to remind myself of a bilingual road sign that I saw on the outskirts of a small town in rural Syria in the mid-1990s: 'Make light speed – place full of inhabitants.' I think that's good advice, folks.